Chapter Three

Pam Oman

Dedicated to my husband Bob who always said I SHOULD write a book, and to my sons and daughters-in-law who always knew I COULD.

October 23, 2013

The End

"There comes a time in a man's life when to get where
he has to--if there are no doors or windows--he walks
through a wall." --Bernard Malamud

It's true as people say, that in those last few moments before death, your whole life passes before you. And as lives go mine was a good one.

Childhood wasn't exactly a storybook one for me, mainly because my dad was an alcoholic. Oh, not the lay-in-the-gutter or couldn't-hold-a-job kind. By the time I came along his drinking was limited to a bout here and there. In between he was a fun, personable guy with a steady job and lots of friends. He was one of those people who "could have sold an igloo to an Eskimo", and would have enjoyed doing so.

My mom and I had a very special relationship. She was one of the kindest, sweetest human beings I ever knew. Probably because of her gentleness she wanted to try to make life for her family as normal as possible, covering for my dad's drinking whenever necessary. She was what we now call the enabler in the alcoholic family, and as one she bore a lot of pain, patiently and without complaint.

Sister Pat and brother Gary, eleven and ten years older than me, experienced the worst of the consequences of my dad's alcoholism. Both reacted with anger and were never able to completely forgive my dad, even in his sober old age. They were both protective of me in their own ways, but as we grew older I was the one who usually reached out to them and arranged family get-togethers. Certainly, today's openness about addiction would have benefitted our family, as would have counseling.

Our family moved often when I was young so I had a hard time making friends. My shyness didn't help either. But by high school I had good friends, both boy and girl. A group of us guys had a little Quonset hut which we hung out at, a rendezvous spot after hunting or a place to play cards. We didn't drink or bring girls there--hard to believe but true.

After one year at a local junior college I transferred to Luther College. The decision to go there affected the rest of my life because early on I met Pam, the love of my life. I'd never felt so comfortable with a girl and soon we were seriously dating. We shared a love of family, faith, music, literature, and the outdoors. I gave her my frat pin one year and a diamond the next, but not after a lot of internal dialogue about the decision to marry.

We were married a month after graduation in a traditional Lutheran church wedding with a reception in the church parlors. We spent our first married night in Hudson, Wisconsin which was a foreshadowing neither of us could have known at the time.

My twenties were spent going in and out of graduate schools which kept me from being in the service during the Viet Nam War years. I finally graduated as a veterinarian when I was thirty years old. By then we had two sons and moved to Rice Lake for my first job in a two-man veterinary practice there. Three years and another son later we moved to Barron where I practiced for nearly thirty years. Oh, how I loved the cows and the farmers! Of course, calls that came in the middle of the night were always tough, especially in the winter when I'd leave our warm bed and Pam who could go back to sleep.

Before having children, I never realized what a joy they would be--they were truly Pam's greatest gift to me. Oh, there were tough times and angry moments, but they knew we loved them unconditionally. That didn't mean we loved everything they did, oh my no! Each had at least one run-in with the law over minor matters, and after having three teenage boys for one year we watched our hair start to gray.

It would be a lie if I said I had anything less than lots of wonderful adventures through the years. Pam gave me pretty much all the rope I wanted so I left home many times to hunt, fish, canoe, and attend vet conventions without her and with my buddies. Of course, the cabin on the lake in Canada was my favorite getaway where I hosted numerous family members and friends in the quiet wilderness.

Later, when the boys were on their own, Pam and I started taking trips together. For several years one or two of our sons worked for an airline, and we were able as parents to fly free or almost so. We took three trips to Italy, and on one ventured into Switzerland, Germany, and France as well. We went around Lake Superior one fall, and made two visits to Montreal and the northeast US. Pam even made sure we got to NYC for about two hours and to Boston for about as long. But the most emotional trip was to Norway and Sweden, the lands of Pam's and my ancestors. We even got to the small island home in Norway's northern ocean waters that my mother's father left when he was twenty years old.

Our Scandinavian trip in 2012 was clouded by my advancing Parkinson's Disease and my withdrawal from a dopamine agonist shortly before the trip. I'll never know how long I'd had Parkinson's (PD) when I was diagnosed in December 2007. Apparently, my long-time lack of sense of smell was an early indicator that my dopamine production was lower than it should be.

My journey with PD was fairly easy at first, although even before diagnosis I noticed a slight left leg tremor, a softer voice, and slowness of movement. I remember telling Pam that a surgery on a cow for a twisted stomach used to take an hour and then it was a two-hour procedure for me. Since there's no definitive test for PD, a neurologist has to make a diagnosis based on clinical signs and by a person's response to dopamine replacement. There was never a problem with my responding well to dopamine, but as time went on I needed more and more of it and at such frequent doses.

When I first attended a presentation about deep brain stimulation surgery (DBS) I was intrigued with the idea. Being a doctor I strongly believed there's a cure for everything, or at least every attempt should be made to cure illnesses. Pam was frightened by the prospect of brain surgery for me, but after research and knowing my feelings about it she got on board with it.

The process of determining whether or not a person can benefit from DBS is a lengthy one. I had put so much hope in the surgery that if I had been denied the chance to have it I would have been devastated. Surgery was scheduled for February, then rescheduled for March 2013. By then my off periods--time when the meds had worn off--were at least half of my waking day, and my nights were often nearly sleepless. Swallowing was difficult so I took pills with applesauce, food and especially protein interfered with my meds' absorption, and often I froze in place unable to move. Asking Pam to help me off the toilet, buckle my belt, or button my shirt was common.

She was a good caregiver, as supportive as I could ask for, and did a great job of learning all she could about PD and keeping me on track for appointments. She prodded me to exercise and get out with people, both of which she knew she needed to encourage. But human being that she is there were times when our life dragged her down. Neither of us envisioned our early retirement this way and without any hope of its getting better.

Well, certainly before DBS and for the first few weeks after it we did have hope that it would be the miracle that many people experience from it. Often patients can reduce their meds and still have very little off time. In my case however, not so. Oh, surgery went well except for the horribly irritating feeling in my left leg during it. I did get to have the so-called honeymoon period for a couple of weeks when I felt almost "normal" again, and then we went for the real test of the system, the first programming.

Now, after four programmers have tried their skill and artistry with the system, the end result is that I find little if any benefit from DBS. The whole process even seems to have left me weaker and more vulnerable than before it. About fifteen to twenty minutes of walking with Pam is the most I can manage. My nights are usually spent on the floor with a pillow, and my drooling is out of control. I've lost weight and eating is problematical. I'm having trouble reading, watching TV, or looking at a computer screen. I know my personality is changing, and that the paranoia I feel will soon damage relationships with those I love. Thinking is fuzzy at times and following even simple instructions is difficult.

I thoroughly enjoyed the prime rib at the meeting of Light and Water Commissioners last night, and surprising myself, took a second helping of it. Pam told me she was proud of me for going to the meeting, but the light at the end of the tunnel has gone out for me. She will find the note in my little book where I wrote, "I love her so much I don't know what to do with myself some times. We have had a special life together." As a veterinarian, I know how we treat an animal who can no longer enjoy life's simple pleasures. Heck, how many times have I looked into a dog's or cat's or cow's eyes -- sometimes those of a beloved pet -- and seen their silent plea to help them out of their predicament?

Pam saves so much stuff so I know she still has, and will always treasure, what I wrote for her in 2009. My words started with, "Then I met Pam at Luther. We had a couple of so-so dates and I remember being at the Union and, we were talking and connecting on several levels, and then I knew that she was the one. I did hang on to the engagement ring for a while just to make sure in my mind that she was the right one. My love for Pam literally gets stronger every day. Finally, we were blessed with three wonderful sons. Each one is his own person, but we love them all very much. I thought I knew how much fun it would be to have

11

kids, but in reality it has meant so much more than I knew. The good things just keep happening. First fantastic wives and then a granddaughter and now two more grandchildren coming on board. To paraphrase a poet: 'Look on my works ye mighty and despair.' Shelley. And then the sands of time covered up King Ozymandias' good works. I suppose the sands of time will get me too. Probably even faster than they did for the good King. Takk for alt."

God is loving and kind, and I know with absolute certainty that He has a better, more glorious life waiting for me on the other side. I will miss my family and friends, the earth and all its wonders, but I go to a new life and new adventures. I know Pam, the boys and our daughters-in-law, our granddaughters, and the extended families will miss me but will be OK. They're strong, and they will support each other. As for me, I know that "even though I walk through the valley of the shadow of death I will fear no evil, for Thou are with me, thy rod and thy staff they comfort me."

"There comes a time in a man's life...he walks through a wall". The wall that Bob could no longer be confined by, or defined by, and so the one he had to walk through was his PD. Some people can live within the walls of debilitating disease, Bob could not. When his swallowing, walking, getting up and down, sleeping, thinking, and emotions had been affected he had to make a decision. He had to take control of a life that now rarely offered him that chance. Several men we knew told me they understood, one even telling me he would hope to be so brave in the same circumstances. Pastor Steve's funeral sermon summed up Bob's life so well and also touched on his death by suicide. He was the first one who met with me in those early morning hours of October 23, saying among many other things that "men are so defined by what they are able to do." As an Army chaplain as well as a pastor and a man, he knew the truth of what he said.

And so, "in the end, only these things matter: how much you loved, how gently you lived, and how peacefully you let go of things not meant for you." --Buddha. Bob had all three.

October 23, 2013

The Beginning

"There will come a time when you believe everything
is finished. That will be the beginning."
--Louis L'Amour

"You can't start the next chapter of your life if you
keep re-reading your last one." --Unknown

Bob had been telling people what a sound sleeper I was, claimed that not even an invading army would wake me. I guess that's what he was counting on the morning of October 23.

About 4:15 am I woke up, not to any particular noise that I was aware of. Often if I wake before getting up in the morning I'll not open my eyes but lie quietly expecting to go back to sleep. This early morning however, I soon blinked and realized the bathroom light was on. This didn't surprise me too much since Bob wasn't in bed. Sleeping for many afflicted with PD is problematic, if not nightmarish as it had become for Bob. He told me that in the last few weeks he'd occasionally taken a bath in the night, hoping to relax and then be able to get to sleep.

Knowing of his night bath taking habit, I assumed that's what he was doing. I lay in bed for maybe twenty minutes and then decided to go check on him. Since his pajamas were on the bedroom floor I wasn't surprised to find he was in the bathtub, unclothed. But my God, if I could wipe one picture from my memory it would be looking at him, perfectly still, with blood under his midsection. I ran to the phone in the kitchen and called 911, not sure of what I said to the woman who answered. She asked if I thought he was dead to which I replied I didn't know. She asked me to check for a pulse which I did go back to do. I felt nothing and reported it to her. After that much of the day is a blur.

Soon there were several police cars at the house, a few officers, and a neighbor and friend who was a retired policeman. The officer in charge wanted the names and addresses of our sons as he said officers would contact police close to their homes and send them to tell our sons that their dad had died. This must be some kind of protocol, not my idea. The one in charge wanted to know who I'd like to have come to be with me. My choice was one of my two pastors who lived nearby. But she was out of town that week, and after what seemed like an eternity someone called our second pastor. I didn't know Pastor Steve well before this, but as an army chaplain and pastor he proved to be a source of great strength for me.

Steve and I sat on the sofa for what seemed hours. It was the curvy, feminine, used leather sofa that my brother and his wife had gifted us with a couple of months earlier. I apologized to Steve for sitting so close to him and at times absentmindedly patting his leg. I'm a touchy-feely person by nature and if ever I needed the comfort that touching gives, it was then. I wrapped myself in the crocheted bedspread my grandma had made which usually hung on the back of the sofa. I know I was shaking and quivering from all the emotion passing through me. The pattern of this spread is called "Selbu Rose" in Norway, and the legend is that anyone covered by it will be warmed.

I didn't do much writing in those first couple of months after Bob died. I'm sure I and most of our immediate family were in shock. Bob's sudden death by suicide caused trauma none of us will ever completely erase. John and Andy were both traveling that day, Andy so far as in South Africa for work, so we were not all together until a few days later. Sons and daughters-in-law, brothers and wives, my niece and nephew, my cousin and his wife, friends, neighbors, and pastors helped make crucial decisions and wrapped me in their blankets of love and support. I know my healing started

18

immediately as I spent the first few nights at my cousin's home an hour from Barron. It's a beautiful home in a wooded setting, at that time of year glorious in its October fall foliage.

Anne Lamott could have been describing me when she wrote about an acquaintance in her book Help, Thanks, Wow. "I have seen many survive unsurvivable losses, and seen them experience happiness again. How is this possible? Love flowed to them from their closest people, and from their community, surrounded them, sat with them, held them, fed them, swept their floors. Time passed. In most cases, their pain evolved slowly into help for others."

During this time, I did however write about what has become my connection to Bob, my reassurance that he is still with me. I will tell of many times when its appearance has given me comfort. Two days after Bob's death I went for a walk, my first in a couple of days. I left my cousin and his wife's house with her instructions to just keep taking right turns, that way I couldn't get lost. This sounded simple, but my interest in looking at homes got me in trouble. I went down several cul de sacs, and after the last one I came back to the main road and turned right, but of course I should have turned left at that point. Soon I was lost—how could this happen? I looked up at the beautiful blue sky and saw a jet stream. My reaction was that there was Bob, gently making fun of me because of my notoriously bad sense of direction. This was the first time I felt I had heard from him since he died; this made sense to me because I figured he would have had a long trip from one life to another. From that moment on I have paid attention to the sky, hoping to feel Bob's presence and knowing that he's still in touch with those of us he left here.

Also, in those first days, I did jot down some of the things people said to me that helped me heal and gave me insight into Bob's suicide. These were people who knew us well so understood the depth of my loss and the shock that Bob's suicide caused. I already mentioned our pastor who sat with me, sharing my pain and shock. He knew that for Bob, a once strong and vital man, life had become a never-ending series of "can-not-dos". A good friend of Bob's hugged me tightly and said, "Pam, I'm so sorry, but I understand why." Simple words, but so much comfort. Another man who enjoyed playing fierce tennis matches with Bob took me aside and said, "Bob was so brave; in his situation, I don't know if I could have done what he was able to do." One of my brothers described Bob as unable to see the light at the end of a black tunnel; another friend said he was in a world he didn't want to be living in.

More words came from the clinical nurse who was part of a support group; she said Bob did a "good thing" based on her experience of caring for people with degenerative diseases. Another nurse who had been part of Bob's care team through the DBS surgery echoed the same sentiment. One friend who worked with depressed patients said that once a person decides to take his life he acts completely normally up to the end. She said this to dismiss any guilt I might have felt for not being able to foresee this and thus prevent his death. Bob had in fact seen a psychiatrist several times over the course of several months. He had said Bob wasn't depressed in any clinical sense, but did need to feel in control of his life. His mindset in his last few weeks would have been as Rollo May described "as the inability to construct a future." A longtime friend to both of us pointed to this characteristic of Bob—his desire to control, to be decisive—as key. Finally, by ending his life, which for months had left him powerless over even the simplest of tasks, he could control it.

The much loved and respected Robin Williams, who also had PD, died by suicide not quite a year after Bob. His widow Susan related in the "Closer Weekly" September 1, 2014 issue: "Ultimately the agony became too great to bear. We may never know what the trigger was when Robin finally decided to leave this world—he loved his kids and friends, and in many ways, he had a great life."

Bob's funeral was the first important matter the family and I had to work on. Surprisingly, we found that there was a therapy in deciding on details and remembering Bob's life which we would be celebrating. And what a life it was! Rich and full in so many ways, and at every turn the good humor that Bob was known for. Several years earlier Bob had written down the music he wanted at his funeral, wishes we honored by asking friends to provide. Andy, Matt, and John wanted to speak about their dad, and I hoped that I would be able to also. Most of what I did was read the last Valentine Bob wrote for me several months before he died and a month before his DBS surgery.

"Pam, we've had a wonderful life together. We can't do all the things we used to do together. But we can choose to be happy or sad. Let's choose to be happy! We have had our trials but most people have. We aren't going to be around forever so let's choose to enjoy the things we can together, things like enjoying time with our kids and their spouses and grandkids. Also, playing Cribbage and Farkel, watching a few TV shows, listening to classical music, visiting with friends and relatives, cross country skiing, walks, snuggling in bed, and whatever else comes our way. Let's choose to have our glass half full and go on from there! Happy Valentine's Day, your loving hubby!"

I ended my words by quoting in Norwegian and translating what Bob's second cousin Astrid from Norway e-mailed me. It translates as, "I'm in God's hands no matter what happens to me." Bob certainly believed this and so do I!

Matt was the first son to talk about Bob, drawing inspiration from the Boy Scout Law which Bob, an Eagle Scout, followed for life. "A Boy Scout is trustworthy, loyal, helpful, friendly, courteous, kind, obedient, cheerful, thrifty, brave, clean, and reverent." Matt recited the words and gave examples of how Bob followed them. John spoke next and used a list the kids had drawn up to honor Bob for his birthday one year; they called the list "Sixty-one Things We Love about Bob". He highlighted Bob's prowess as a veterinarian, his enthusiasm for and loyalty to his favorite sports teams, even when losing, and his love of a good joke and self-deprecating humor. Andy, who couldn't be with the rest of the family for a few days because of a business trip, said he had done a lot of thinking about his dad once he heard the devastating news of his death. He knew how Bob loved poetry, and to remember him had picked to read the poem "A Thing of Beauty" by John Keats. The ending lines are, "We have imagined for the mighty dead; An endless fountain of immortal drink, Pouring unto us from the heaven's brink." They encircled each other as they spoke, and all three thanked Bob for being their dad, and sent him their love.

After the funeral, friends, and especially family who were also grieving, were generous and loving in their support for me. Andy took me for a walk in a beautiful wildlife preserve near his Bloomington home. I was excited to find abundant Bittersweet which we picked to preserve. Bob had told me how scarce this plant was in the wooded areas he knew, so finding that here it was almost an invasive species was amazing. Matt and I went to a suicide survivor's support group in his hometown of Woodbury. We found that several who were there were far less healed, some after several years, than we felt. We attributed that to our amazing support system. Since John lived in Hudson he knew the city and contacted a good friend who was a realtor to be on the lookout for the kind of simple, one level home I was interested in buying. And daughters-in-law Sarah, Janna, and Jenna wrapped me in their wonderful warmth. They made a cozy spot in their homes for me and graciously invited me to stay whenever I wanted or needed to.

Quite quickly life returned, not to the old normal, but to a new normal without Bob. I went back to church, back to my volunteering at school, back to helping my ninety-year-old mom maintain her life in her own home. We never told her how Bob died, and she never asked. Did she maybe intuit the answer? She and Bob often appeared to be on the same wavelength. She also saw how weakened Bob's physical condition was, how he had

22

"failed" in her word, and how "sick" he was at times. For me, as one care taking job ended another became more necessary because mom had suffered her first stroke several months earlier.

Looking back, I think closing the chapter of my life in Barron started shortly after Bob died. Our life there was built on his being in veterinary practice and our sons growing into adults in this safe, small town environment. I had made a home for them, helped with the vet practice, encouraged them, and filled in the details of our lives. But with Bob gone and the boys grown and married, I felt like I was on a branch of a slowly withering tree. By Christmas I was certain I would move so the three sons' families spent the holiday with me in Barron, our last one there.

Shortly after Christmas, our first without Bob and my last in Barron, I put my feelings about him into a little tribute to him. I hoped, and I thought, that he would approve of it.

The heavenly father spoke to you

And said, you've done your best.

You fought the fight you couldn't win

And now you need your rest.

I'll lead you safely home to heaven

To be with all the blest.

You'll leave behind an empty space

Within the Oman nest,

But they will hear and then live out

The words of your request:

"Be honest, kind, and generous,

And loyal to your team.

Work hard, play harder, love God and each other.

Do this and you will pass life's final test."

On January 4, 2014, I wrote in my journal that it was my most lonesome day yet. Perhaps it was triggered by seeing the Facebook picture of cousin Anne and Andrea who were married today. They're so happy with each other. Of course, I have to remember that Bob and I shared many years together, and those years were mostly good ones. The last couple of rough years can't negate all the fun we had and the great relationship we had, starting when we were only nineteen years old. But the hole in my heart created by his passing will never heal, and it shouldn't. I keep rereading the words in a pamphlet about grief given to me by a friend that say, "We never get over the death of a loved one. Grief lasts a lifetime. It is a process of acknowledging that life has changed and finding ways to live with the change. Just as our love continues, so does our grief." Or in the words of a favorite writer, Anne Lamott, "You will lose someone you can't live without, and your heart will be badly broken, and the bad news is that you never completely get over the loss of your beloved. But this is also the good news. They live forever in your broken heart that doesn't seal back up. And you come through. It's like having a broken leg that never heals perfectly—that still hurts when the weather gets cold, but you learn to dance with the limp."

January 30. Today I made granola and found much in my cupboards has gotten old and out of date—it's hard to find the living among so much that is dead. Is this why I want to move away from Barron so quickly?

Today when I talked to mom she thought my dad had just died, actually he's been gone for almost fourteen years. Maybe she's confusing my dad and Bob as she's having more frequent delusions. For her, as for Bob, these delusions are her reality and not to be argued about. It's hard to keep my sanity when faced as I was with Bob's PD and death and now mom's post-stroke life. Yet, hard as it is, I must hang on to my own life—I have to be more than a care giver. I sometimes think I'm supposed to be with mom and give her a life, but I can't let go of who I am again after it

24

happened two years ago with Bob. I have to be with my kids and grandkids and see that there is life and hope, the future.

Church choir director David called with news of the In Memory of Bob music he found – "I Want to Be a Witness for my Lord", a jazzy spiritual. Oh, Bob would love it! David said we will sing it later in the spring.

February 5. This is John's thirty-fifth birthday, one of my hardest days yet. We wish Bob were here to join in another family celebration, and especially in this year of the Paralympics in Sochi, Russia. Last week the list of US athletes going to Sochi was released. Finally, the reality of John's competing started to sink in when I read his name among the sixteen named to the US team. Bob did know that John would be competing in the world championships in Canmore, Canada, and felt quite certain that he'd also be going to Sochi. Bob's spirit will be with John as he competes, inspiring him to do his best. And there are other family members, now deceased, who would have been so proud of John and his accomplishments—my dad, Bob's dad and mom, many of our aunts and uncles and grandparents, and on and on. How fitting with our heritage that he's competing in Nordic skiing!

I'm rereading Joan Didion's <u>The Year of Magical Thinking</u> with a totally different view point than my first reading several years ago. She writes about her first year of grieving after her husband's death and of the very physical and mental effects of grief—hopefully this is what explains my forgetfulness of words I occasionally can't retrieve, my lack of concentration, my tiredness in the morning. Yesterday I got a call from Lorraine, another recent widow. She's eighty-six and doing quite well after her husband's slow decline and death due to Alzheimer's.

Leona is another friend of mine, in her nineties, and widowed for nearly thirty-four years after her husband had coffee in a hotel cafe and contracted Legionnaires' Disease. He suffered for eight weeks and died at the early age of sixty. Who said life is fair? We're not given any guarantees when we're born. I move between feelings of Bob's having lived a long, good life filled to the brim, and that of his spirit and enjoyment having been cut so short by his PD. That's the tragedy in his situation, the disease itself and possibly the surgery to help it. DBS surgery was his only hope of finding relief from the symptoms of PD but was perhaps what sent him on a more rapid downward spiral. We'll never know.

I could not pity him, I could not. He was so vulnerable, so helpless at times, that he seemed almost childlike. I may have appeared like a parent to him, not a spouse or equal. But that too was because of PD, not his personality. We had lost the real Bob, the fighter for the underdog, the competitor, and found in his place a weakened, dispirited man, aged way beyond his sixty-seven years. Forgive me if I should have pitied him, especially when he would say, "Can't you see what a mess I am?" Of course, I could, but what would it have helped him for me to agree and add to his hopelessness.

A couple days ago I reached in the pocket of a jacket of his and found two paper towels that he would have used to catch his drool or wipe it up. This was yet another of the quality of life issues that were so troublesome for him. He had to be concerned with swallowing, eating—what and when—sleeping (forget it), talking; the rest of us take these acts of daily living for granted. Yet, I could not, would not pity him. "Pity, it's curable" an ad for a children's hospital says.

My magical thinking was that I didn't want to, I couldn't, face the reality of Bob's decline. I kept trying to be the voice of optimism, the glass half full. Bob and I traded places in this respect, once in a while his maintaining the optimism and saying I wasn't. I will forever ask myself if I was supposed to have been more realistic with him, agreeing with him when he would point out his frailty and decline and fear of soon needing to live in a care facility.

February 6. Today I went to the Parkinson's Support Group in Shell Lake, the one Bob and I had attended for several years, and had the feeling that in a way I didn't belong there anymore. Again, there was reinforcement of my thinking that Bob had progressed more in his PD than the other people there have. Or at the least he couldn't cope with his PD like the others can. That was always a question in my mind—is it truly worse for him or did he handle the symptoms differently than others did? I always felt he was so fortunate to not have any pain and no arthritis—what a miracle that would be for me! If he hadn't been so self-conscious, so self-absorbed, in later months, could he have gained power over his PD and had an easier time being with people?

February 9. Pastor Lori spoke today on the text from Matthew that we are to be "the salt of the earth, the light to the world". She explained the meaning of the text as God's having transformed us into saints who are on our way home. I love that image of all of us being on our way home. Home, such a hard place to find in this world—maybe that's why I like Lori's idea of being on a path to a "heavenly" home.

Clearly, I have decided that I will be leaving Barron. I haven't once questioned the decision made so quickly after Bob died. I have a need to clean out every box and corner and drawer. Is it duty, or prudence knowing I will move, or obsession? The house cleaning does make me feel better, freer, and with a sense of accomplishment. Am I over doing it? Moving too fast? Anne Lamott has said, "If we stay where we are, where we're stuck, where we're comfortable and safe, we die there. When nothing new can get in, that's death. But new is scary, and new can be disappointing, and confusing—we had this all figured out, and now we don't." Confusing, most certainly!

February 12. This afternoon when I was downtown I saw a man come out of the bakery. I would guess he was in his late seventies, but impossible to know. He walked or shuffled very slowly and had no expression on his face. I didn't recognize him so could not be certain if he had PD, but he reminded me so much of how Bob looked and moved most of the time in later months. No wonder our sons said they found it difficult to believe Bob was

27

only sixty-seven when they compared him to other men, healthy men, his age. Again, that terrible nagging question of should I have done more feeling sorry for him, pitying him? That's the fine line I walked as his wife and care giver.

February 14. Valentine's Day, but I had forgotten that until I was driving to Eau Claire to visit my mom. Remembering the date, I thought how wonderful it would be if Bob could have wished me Happy Valentine's Day. I turned to look out my side window and there to the east was a jet stream, my avatar for Bob. This was the first time that I was able to "summon him" or find the stream when I wanted or needed to. He was most definitely sending me love and Valentine greetings. It was Carla who long ago told me about a friend who lost her young daughter in an accident, and was helped by deciding on a symbol of her, something that would remind her of her daughter. For me it is so comforting to see the jet stream and think it is Bob communicating with me.

February 20. This is the first time I actually made a meal for myself. Snow was coming down and I thought chili would be so good to make and eat. Of course, my two and a half hours of outside activity meant I was hungrier than usual! This afternoon I visited again with Leona—what a joy she is. She's ninety-four and mentally sharp. She said she wakes up every morning and says a thank you to God prayer for keeping her through the night. She prays several times during the day, often for other people, and added that she had prayed for me. She wanted the dates of the Paralympics to put them on her calendar so she could try to watch them on TV, hoping to see John compete. It's strange how often I find other women whom I so admire or bond with. I love my mom but have never had chemistry with her. It wouldn't be surprising if I've spend much of my life searching for other mother figures.

Dotty underwent her second surgery today, again to relieve the pressure that bleeding in the brain was causing. My prayers are with her, my guardian angel in those days after Bob died. Her struggle and recovery after suffering a brain aneurysm led me to thoughts of Bob. He always wanted to leave the party before it was even close to being over. On that score, we were exact opposites as I always want to stay until the end. So, his final decision, his last act, was to insure that he could leave the party before it was over. Or, maybe more accurately, for him with PD, the party was over. And who can judge, in his situation many of us would maybe like to leave before the inevitable bitter end.

The Olympics, which precede the Paralympics, have begun. A side bar to the activities was an interview with the parents of Sarah Burke, 1982 – 2012. She worked to insure that the women's halfpipe snowboarding event would become an Olympic event. She died performing her event, but yet her mother could say, "I thought the worst thing would be to lose Sarah, and then I realized the worst would be to never have had her." Let that be my feelings about Bob, the worst would have been to never have had him in my life. Another skier said of her, "She loved life, and lived it to the fullest." So, did Bob, until PD prevented him from living it to the fullest, and that's what he couldn't endure.

February 23. A conversation I had with one of my daughters-in-law may have shed some light on the nature of Bob's and my relationship as he became more affected by his PD. We were talking about shielding children from danger or harm when I realized that's what I had done for Bob for much of our life together. I shielded him from his work at times by taking the phone off the hook when he was on call, or making him sound more unavailable than he was. I sometimes explained his not so tactful behavior to whoever he had a problem with, often family members or good friends. I never talked negatively about him to anyone else. I kept my kids quiet at night and was always the one who got up with them when they were sick or had trouble sleeping. I had meals ready when he wanted to eat and kept the house stocked with food he liked. This list could go on. What I couldn't shield him from was the effects of his PD. I tried to stay positive, often denying that PD was making life difficult for him. I couldn't make PD go away however, and since he never knew how much interference I had run for him, he thought I had changed when I could no longer make life with PD easy for him. This is probably why at times he thought my attitude toward him had changed—no, I had only run into the brick wall of PD.

February 25. Facebook articles posted on a Parkinson's website provided scary reading for me. In "Medscape" was the article titled "Parkinson's Disease Surgery Linked to Increased Suicide Risk". From it I quote, "This further suggests that an induced disturbance of the basal ganglion circuitry, presumably in the limbic component, may induce mood disorders and/or suicidal ideas." This was the area of the brain where Bob's electrode was implanted. And from an article in "Clinical Psychiatry News" was the information that the suicide rate in the first ten months after undergoing DBS surgery was eleven to thirty-seven times higher in PD patients than in the general population. The survey yielding this information was taken from seventy-five centers which performed DBS surgeries. Again, that nagging awful thought that the surgery Bob had pinned all his hopes on was what further debilitated him and perhaps even made him suicidal.

Another book I reread is Anna Quindlen's One True Thing, a story about a daughter who gives up her career to come home to take care of her mother suffering from incurable cancer. The book highlights the struggles of being a care taker, but also shows the reader the terrible reality of the mother who is living with such a debilitating illness. Finally, unknown to anyone else, the mother takes her life by slowly stockpiling enough of her morphine to give herself a fatal dose. She too decided that life under certain conditions is not worth living. Maybe this woman, like Bob, had lost hope, which "is a funny thing. It's not like love, or fear, or hate. It's a feeling you don't really know until it's gone." Taken from another Quindlen book, Still Life With Bread Crumbs.

Should I wonder why I am so distracted and lack concentration? Dotty's slow recovery from her stroke, mom's failing health and increasing dementia, John's going to Russia amid fears of security issues, losing Bob, thinking about buying a house in Hudson. Daily life in Barron must go on as well as I try to keep up with my commitments to church, school, friends, and family not in Barron. One little thing goes wrong, like the garage door opener breaking or this never-ending winter bringing more snow, and life seems overwhelming.

Anne Lindbergh, wife of the famous pilot Charles, wrote Gift from the Sea in which she finds lessons in the different sea shells gathered on the beach. She describes middle age when the children are grown and gone as the time that "one cannot go back to that tightly closed world. One has grown too big, too many sided, for that rigidly symmetrical shell. I am not sure that one has not grown too big for any shell at all. She points out that certain times in life "one might be free for growth of mind, heart, and talent; free at last for spiritual growth." Is there where I am now?

February 28 (Bob would have been sixty-eight today). One never can predict where a sudden burst of support might come from. This afternoon the local florist delivered a beautiful bouquet with an enclosed card reading, "Thoughts with you during this day and the days ahead, in memory of Bob-- Maureen." A friend had remembered that this was Bob's birthday and knew it would be an emotionally hard day for me. Thank you! I will enjoy the roses now and dry them as an everlasting bouquet.

Mom called three times today, leaving two messages before I answered her the third time. She's having a very confusing day, wondering how "we folks" were, and saying that no one had come home for supper yet at her house. The report about Dotty's condition is that her progress is two steps forward, one step backward, the continuing problem being the headaches. The angiogram showed there's pressure from excess fluid causing the headaches; the hope is that draining this can relieve them. Losing

Bob, slowly and then permanently, Mom's deteriorating physical and mental states, and Dotty's fragility are all so destabilizing.

My hope is that I can be strong enough emotionally to maintain myself. I need strength to settle the questions of where I will live, when I will move, will and when this house sell. I truly think that until I have left my life in Barron and found a new one I won't be able to be whole. I was a part of the life here, maybe the lesser half, and in another situation, I will be the whole life. This maybe makes sense only to me; there's no voice of Bob to lead me in any of this.

I put in a CD I hadn't played in months and soon heard the song "Teach Your Children Well". This was the song the three boys wove through the video about their memories of all the good times spent at the little cabin Bob and his two friends built in Canada. Andy, Matt, and John had made the video and accompanying book for Bob's birthday, his last it turned out. The day was within weeks of his DBS surgery when he had very little "on" time even with his taking medication every two hours. His capacity to enjoy anything, not even this precious video shown on Matt and Janna's big TV screen, had disappeared. We had all been so sure this surprise would have been a big emotional hit for Bob, but if it was he couldn't express it.

March 3. Support can come from unexpected sources and so can inspiration. I watched most of the Academy Awards and paid particular attention to Robert and Kristin Lopez, the writers of the songs in the Disney movie "Frozen". They wanted to write songs that "would instill in them (daughters Katie and Annie) the idea that shame and fear should not prevent them from being the magical people that they really are." This should be the goal of all of us parents, grandparents, teachers--all of us who help raise children. I will try to remember this!

March 6. It's easy to remember how difficult daily living had become for Bob. Swallowing was hard so he took his medication with applesauce, a tip he learned at a PD support group meeting. Eating was hard to manage because any proteins eaten take precedence over dopamine in the digestive tract. For instance, eating a chicken breast would negate the effectiveness of the next pill he would take. Today a farmer I talked to was remembering how quite a few years ago Bob was struggling on a call at his farm, finding it exhausting to pack up his gear after doing a surgery or other procedure. This was even before Bob had been diagnosed with PD. The farmer, eight years older than Bob, thought Bob was the older man. His eyesight had worsened to the point that our eye doctor told me that Bob was struggling at his last eye appointment in September. Using the computer, reading, and watching TV had all become difficult for him. But again, I couldn't give in to the darkness and tell him how hopeless he was. This to me is the crux of a care giver's dilemma. I believe that person must be the source of hopefulness, the courage, the will to go on—in the end my efforts didn't succeed in convincing him that his life should go on as it was.

March 7. When visiting mom today I had the deja vu moment I would not have wanted. She had been invited to go to a fish fry supper with a friend but turned down the offer. She said she always feels so "dumb" when with other people. She also said she gets so nervous getting ready to leave the house with someone. Of course, this reminded me of Bob in his last months. He had an increasing resistance to be with people, citing his off meds feeling as the reason. For both of them the cause is no doubt the changes in their brains and an understandable concern. Yet, every piece of advice mandates that a person stay involved and socially connected. Again, the dilemma of the care taker who should try to help a person do what is best for him or her.

This was especially a problem for me with Bob since his social life and mine were so intertwined. Not only did he have increasing reluctance to leave home, but he wanted me with him and was almost childlike at times in his dependence on me. But when I tried to express my occasional need to be independent of him, he resented it and thought I didn't have any sympathy for him. His and mom's feelings of inadequacy at meeting their own needs are only strengthened by their reliance on someone else to help them. It's another of those no-win dilemmas that never get addressed in the advice for care givers.

March 11. While driving home today I realized that grief is more than emotional; it's physical as well. I was missing Bob, mourning his loss, in my gut, viscerally. This must be akin to tasting a color or an odor. I knew I wanted him there with me physically—my thoughts and memories of him weren't enough to fill the void I felt today.

Meriting a journal entry today is the fact that I talked to Joel who said he and his wife want to buy my house! This is a small miracle that will save me the stress of getting the house ready to sell or doing anything to make it more likely to sell. It means however that in a way I'm a homeless person because I haven't found a place to buy in Hudson. This does give me some leeway with money concerns, more free to think about hiring movers, redecorating a different home, and not worrying about finding a source of tax free money to buy another home. So, thank you Joel and Janelle!

Bob, I couldn't be doing this on my own if we hadn't decided several years ago that one day we would move closer to our kids and families. Lately though I couldn't imagine how we could relocate and try to fit into a new place. It was hard enough for you to be with people who knew you well and accepted your PD. I questioned what kind of social life we would have had where few knew us. I feared, as probably you did, that you were not far from life in a nursing home, or at least from needing help come into our home. Oh again, the tragedy that PD was for you.

March 24. I spent a wonderful weekend with family, celebrating John's joyous return from the Paralympics in Russia and Janna's birthday. Last year March 26, her birthday, was taken up with Bob's surgery. Oh, how hopeful we all were that day and for a couple weeks following. Yesterday everyone was healthy; we ate, and laughed, and watched basketball and the movie "Frozen".

Today I talked to Tony, our city treasurer, who said I should gladly accept an offer on my house that falls a bit below the estimated fair market value. Here in Barron with its low rate of people moving in, that kind of sale is common. I talked to Joel later in the afternoon and we both agreed we want to make this sale work. Soon after that conversation I arrived at church for a meeting and saw four jet streams at once! Never have I seen that happen—thank you Bob, I know you would approve of the sale.

March 25. I feel like I'm standing in two worlds, one with Bob and one without him. It's spooky and lonesome, but in a way so full of opportunity. I'm a little bit like a young girl starting all over. What I need is empowerment so I can move forward with my life. Andy said he's sure it's not an easy transition, this living without Bob and grieving the terrible loss. He said it must be hard to take on all the decision making alone after sharing the job with Bob for my entire adult life. He added that he and Matt and John and their wives love me and support me and stand ready to help however they can. Sarah told me that this making choices for only me is new; I should be confident in knowing myself and what I want and need. Perhaps to boost my confidence she said that I should be so proud of my sons; she knows she will be thrilled if her children can turn out as well as mine did.

April 2. This was another family filled weekend with brothers, kids, grandkids, and a visit to brother-in-law Gary, daughter Brenda, and friend Carole. It seems that given Gary's failing health all three Oman siblings will have passed within less than two years of each other, all with neurological problems of one sort or another.

Mom seemed about like usual when I was with her Saturday to have her tax return done. Even Sunday she sounded good when she called me. Monday not so good however, since she called me at 7 pm to say no one had called her all day; fact was that I had a long phone conversation with her about 4:30 pm. Tuesday evening I called her as soon as I got home from a meeting; she knew that Carla had picked her up but couldn't remember where they'd gone or who they had seen. Wow, there are getting to be bigger and more disturbing holes in her memory. I wonder if one can be drawn into someone else's mental problems. It's easy for me to feel like I'm the one going crazy, first as Bob's condition worsened, and now with mom's increasing dementia. On the other hand, it's so refreshing to be with my young grandkids or with the fourth graders in the classroom where I'm a volunteer. Being with them or other family members and friends reminds me of my sanity; getting outside, walking, using my mind, all help to keep me centered.

April 9. This is a day of scattered thoughts and lack of concentration. Most days I can function well, contributing to family, friends, community, and church. I keep moving forward with my plans to relocate to Hudson, and have now gotten an actual offer to purchase my home here. Yet at times like this I question whether I can begin to accomplish all that I'm trying to do. I wonder if I should simply be staying in Barron, maintaining the status quo, making the easiest choice. My hope is that once I have moved and am settled I can at least quit pondering these questions and move forward with my newly single life. I need to be gentle with myself, accepting that losing Bob and now the "essence" of my mom due to her stroke are negatively affecting my emotional stability. Although my sons and daughters-in-law are so gentle with me and supportive of me I don't want to burden them with my neediness.

Can I have perhaps gotten past the worst of my grieving? I can hold a thought longer and am able to concentrate better. Next week this might be different yet again. I'm so positive about my decision to move to Hudson; several of my friends have said they see God's hand in this. I hope they're right! Today's Wordsmith quote was one that I have had on my refrigerator door for years. Leonardo da Vinci said, "As a well spent day brings happy sleep, so life, well used brings happy death." He lived from 1452 to 1519 which made him, when he died, sixty-seven years old—what a coincidence, exactly Bob's age when he died. Certainly, a parallel can be drawn between the two men, both with so many talents and interests, true "Renaissance men". The extent of Bob's interests and his passion in pursuing them becomes more evident to me as I sort through all of our stuff. From sports to nature, medicine, and music, history, travel, and reading, coin collecting, gardening, playing cards—he enjoyed them all.

To realize how limited his ability to enjoy his passions in his last months is to understand why he quit fighting PD. His last great hope had been the brain surgery, and when, after seeing the fourth programmer, it didn't improve his quality of life, the flame died within him. But this hopelessness about his life was what I could not give in to for his sake, and mine. I tried to keep his glass at least a little full instead of empty. My generally optimistic outlook coupled with what I thought was kindness toward him kept me from acknowledging the direness of his situation. The problem this caused for our relationship was that he could interpret my attitude as a kind of callousness toward him, a non-sympathetic kind of care giving. This was not so—if I could have helped bear his burden or make life better for him I would have. I had always "had his back", tried to smooth the road for him and keep him happy. Now, in the face of PD I was helpless to change anything. Perhaps his occasional frustration with me was actually his frustration with the ravages of PD. I knew without a doubt how much he loved and needed me, and I'm sure he knew how much I loved him.

April 17. I spent several minutes looking at the picture of the two of us that's now hanging in the hall. Bob is smiling broadly and looks ready to crack a good joke. THAT is the Bob I so miss and so loved—but again, that's what I couldn't tell him in the last months because, through no fault of his own, he was so different, so aged, so diminished, so ghostly. Jodi Picoult's description of a character in her book The Storyteller is hauntingly identical to how I could have described Bob. She writes, "He couldn't follow a conversation without his eyes going distant; his muscles had atrophied; he shuffled instead of striding. It was as if he's been bleached of color by harsh experience; and although you could discern the outline of the man he'd been, he was no more substantial than a ghost."

April 29. Today I saw Pastor Lori and last week saw Pastor Steve. There will always be strong bonds between each of the pastors and me. For Steve, it is because of those first hours on October 23 that he spent with me. He ministered to me then and in his conducting Bob's funeral in such a strong, beautiful way; I credit him with making Bob's shocking death somewhat understandable. I gave him the old porcelain bowl that was used to hold the water when Bob was baptized as a baby. I hoped Steve would use it when performing the washing of feet ceremony, Jesus' example of servant hood. Lori was out of town until the day of the funeral, sparing her from what would maybe have been emotionally devastating for her. She, Bob, and I had grown close during our days of work as BeFrienders at church. In our visit today we cried, prayed, talked, and hugged. She told me about her 101-year-old grandmother, now living in a nursing home but intact mentally. She will start wearing a brace for her scoliosis, a condition I've had since my youth. I gave Lori several of Bob's books showing his varied interests, two rocks from his collection, a "peace pen" from Oslo's Nobel Center, and two cotton towels for drying feet after washing them. She had washed mine in our recent Maundy Thursday service, was my servant then and forever will be.

Both Lori and Steve were servants to me, a role I hope to be able to play in other people's lives. I read both of them the words of one of my favorite hymns, "The Servant Song" by Richard Gillard. All the words are powerful, but some of my favorites are, "We are pilgrims on a journey; we're together on this road. We are here to help each other, walk the mile and bear the load. I will weep when you are weeping; when you laugh, I'll laugh with you. I will share your joy and sorrow till we've seen this journey through.

Brother, sister, let me serve you, let me be as Christ to you; pray that I may have the grace to let you be my servant too."

Grieving is such an emotional and also physical process. As I looked at the picture of us at John and Jenna's wedding, one that is of our heads only as we share a kiss, my stomach turned. I so miss the real Bob, the warm and loving Bob, the one free of his PD and its paranoia and at times blue moods.

As I go through our belongings, our thirty-five years of living at 240, I feel like I'm stripping furniture of many layers of finish or peeling an onion. I dig deeper and find evidence of the different stages of our lives, our varying interests, what we found important in years past. Viewed from this vantage point years later, many of the things have lost their value—what I once treasured now I can easily live without. I'm promising to live the last third of my life in a simpler way, not collecting trinkets, not piling layer upon layer. So help me God!

May 16. I haven't written for so long, but not because of lack of emotion or thought. This weekend the three boys were here; it was a busy time and emotionally hard for them and me. As I box up my life my moods go up and down. I'm deconstructing my life of forty-five married years, knowing that I will have to give birth to a new person once I've settled in Hudson. The verse in a devotional booklet I read said, "Do not fear change, for I am making you a new creation, with old things passing away and new things continually on the horizon." And that's the name of the paint color I've chosen for every room in my house in Hudson, HORIZON. I'm scared and excited, sad and happy, overwhelmed and confident. My very great fear is not that I can't take my life apart, but can I put it back together again?

The reason for my lack of writing was that between the last two entries I found and purchased a home in Hudson, no small accomplishment. John's realtor friend had shown me several places at different times, but none had seemed "right". On May 2, Dotty's birthday, we saw one house in the morning and went for a birthday celebration lunch. When we were eating, the realtor called to say he had another new listing to show me, one he thought I would be very interested in seeing. We were there within an hour and found out that there were already two more parties interested in viewing it. As soon as I walked in I was certain it was the one for me. It was about fifteen years old, well taken care of although packed with belongings of the couple and their young daughter who lived there. The paint colors were wild, the flooring needed replacing, and the furniture placement was all wrong, but the flow of the 1272 square feet with a cathedral ceiling was what I wanted. Dotty and I went to the realty office to put in an offer; as the agent was writing it up he said two other offers were coming in. It was to be a cash deal so I had to prove the money was in the life insurance account opened when Bob died. The sellers accepted my slightly over asking price offer, and closing was set for June 19. Wow, I'm not homeless anymore!

May 31. I can't believe how hard this moving process is. As Joel and JeNel put in the garden in my old house, their new house, I likened moving to turning over the soil in the garden. It's hard work, but necessary for new growth. Last night I took down the sign Bob had made years ago with his new router, the sign with the names Andy, Matt, John on it. Even holding it brought a flood of tears and emotions. Yesterday I said good-bye to the kids at school where I volunteer. I compared their move to middle school in the fall to my move out of Barron to Hudson; we're all both scared and excited. I hope to always have a part in children's lives, our future and our hope.

Last weekend I traveled to McFarland to be with cousins Anne and Mary. It provided a wonderful chance to bond with them and to recharge my batteries before my move. We visited their aunt Corinne who had moved last year at age eighty-four to a townhouse there. We had dinner with Paula and Marcus in their vibrant, lovely home, filled with boys so like ours was. Mary and Anne gave me crochet and violin "lessons", reminders that I want to continue learning and using my mind. Mary recently self-published a book providing me with inspiration to do the same. I hope I can do it—I must do it!

June 10. Moving day is fast approaching, less than a week away. John, Jenna, and Andy were here on Saturday, and we all worked hard. I asked the men to decide what they wanted to do with Bob's things, clothes, sporting goods, hunting gear, books and so much more. I know this is emotionally rough for them also, reliving pastimes with Bob and their lives in this house, the whole thirty-five years disappearing except for the memory of it. My toughest moment yet was standing crying with Andy before he left. But I said we were crying because we had such a wonderful life here, one that many people never get to have. Good-bye Barron, you have been good to us.

Appearing in the June 11, 2014 issue of the Barron weekly newspaper was a thank you I wanted to write. It said, "It is with mixed emotions that I'm packing my things to move out of Barron after living here thirty-five years. Barron County, the city, the school system, Barron Community Center, First Lutheran Church, and many friends have cared for us, protected us, educated us, provided work and recreation for us—in short given us such a good life. Bob and our three sons would concur with me in saying we're proud to have called Barron our home. I leave our house in the care of a young man who grew up next door and his family. And I go to Hudson to be nearer to family and not so far from Barron that I can't come back to visit. Thank you everyone, or in Norwegian, "Takk for alt"!

Today I visited with mom, certain that each time I'm with her is another good-bye of sorts. She's as fragile as Bob was, as prone to paranoia, sadness, and lonesomeness as he was near the end. Perhaps her dopamine is almost gone as was his. Yet, as with him, I cannot pity her, nor am I able to give her a life. That is the lesson I have learned over and over, whether with a sibling, spouse, parent, child, or friend. No, each person must make his own life, find his own happiness and reason for being. With both Bob and mom that is probably the crux of their sadness, that there is no longer any reason for them to be here. They know they're loved, but with their capabilities so exhausted they run into their uselessness at every corner. God gave Bob the courage to come home early, for mom it won't end the same. Peace to both of them.

June 11. This evening Lynn hosted a good-bye party for me. We talked, laughed, hugged, and shared great memories. The party was tinged with sadness of course, the struggle Bob faced with PD, and now my leaving Barron. One friend told me I'm the strongest person she knows; I pray every day for the strength to carry on. Another friend cried as she told me that I'd showed her that no matter how much "badness" there is, we must just get up in the morning and live our life. Another friend kissed me and said she and her husband will come visit me in Hudson. I hope many people will!

June 12. Today I talked with Ida Peterson, another recent widow. Her husband Ken was a retired farmer who had used Bob's services as a veterinarian. As church BeFrienders, Bob and I had ministered to Ken and Ida once he had started living in a nursing home. Ken had multiple health problems and in his last days had reacted badly to a drug which was supposed to help minimize his delusions. Finally, he simply quit eating; both men had such a strong faith in God that they could let go of their lives here knowing the next life would be better. Also, by choosing death, they could be in control of their lives which had gone out of control. Many call this bravery. Ida and I said that in hindsight we could see that the men were slowly letting go of their earthly lives—they showed less and less interest in what they had once so enjoyed, like following their favorite sports teams, or being involved in the life of their families. Ida heard my story of the jet stream which reminds me of Bob, and said she would always think of him when she sees it.

June 16. This would have been our forty-sixth wedding anniversary, this year moving van day. Matt surprised me by

42

arriving at 8 am to help get me through the process of clearing out 240 Cityview. The semi arrived and we wondered, too much room or too little? It's mine to use for two weeks so we will use it whatever the case. Our BeFriender friends came at noon with lunch, and also my brother Vern and wife Dixie who share this as their anniversary also. The two movers worked quickly, and by 2:30 everything was loaded with only about two feet to spare. As I left town, I noticed Don Peterson, one of Bob's vet partners, behind me, turning in at the Veterinary Clinic, a nostalgic farewell to Barron. I dropped off our rented TV and internet equipment in Rice Lake, looked at my watch to realize it was 4:00, the time our wedding had started. I shed lots of tears as I drove north to Shell Lake to spend the night with Vern and Dixie.

June 17. The closing on my Barron house went well, as planned. Joel and JeNel still seem thrilled to be moving here. As I looked around the empty house one more time, I thought it looked smaller, and without any furniture a bit like a treehouse. There were more Barron good-byes, a trip to Matt and Janna's for supper, and on to Andy and Sarah's for the night.

June 19. Yesterday granddaughter Elsa, my oldest who will be in first grade in the fall, spent the day with me. Today was the closing on the house in Hudson. There were no problems with this one either, and so far, no "buyer's remorse". I'm anxious for the cosmetic work to begin on my twin home, walls painted and flooring replaced. I wondered today if this is the real me or someone pretending to be me—I hope it's the former. I think I can accomplish this, and have the distinct feeling that for the first time in my life I have truly come home.

June 27. Today was perhaps the hardest day to date in the moving process. It's maybe because I have what now is a rare headache, not the case for much of my life, and work on the new house is moving so slowly. The air is humid which is slowing the setting up of the vinyl floor glue, the painter needs the floor done before he can start, the lawn didn't get mowed...Reminder to self:

NEVER do this again! No one said moving would be easy, and it is not! Janna said however that I've adjusted so well to all the changes, starting with Bob's death. I chose to move on—what other choice is there? And, as I sat on the curb in front of my house realizing again how close I am to all my sons and families, I was thrilled and excited to be here.

Physically and emotionally as hard as my move has been for me, I have been reminded often about what my ancestors went through in their moves from one country, Norway, to a new home in America. In preparation for our second trip to Norway in 2012, I did some research into Bob's and my genealogy and the lives of our ancestors. I found great-great-grandmother Kari who married Samuel, had daughter Sena, and then was widowed when he was killed by a runaway horse. She remarried, had more children, but had to leave Sena behind when the family emigrated. Great grandparents Gulianne and Mathias suffered a horrible loss when they left Norway with three-year-old and fourteen-month-old children. The boat trips usually took several weeks; people were living in crowded conditions with limited food and often stormy weather. During the trip the young son died of illness, and his little body had to be committed to the sea for burial. Great grandmother Karen experienced the class discrimination that was common in those days. Because her family was poor, even needing to beg for food, she was denied an education by those in the upper class who had influence and power.

The stories of two families are especially poignant and tragic. First is Berte's story, second oldest child of Ingebor, the only heir of the beautiful, productive farm called "Apland", and Ole who had married her. Ole was a terrible manager who eventually gambled away the farm, leaving the family only enough leverage to book passage on a ship to America. Berte and a sister followed their parents to Wisconsin where she met and married Tory Olson. In 1861 Tory moved his family to the more fertile soil and greater farming opportunity in southern Minnesota. This was about a year before the Sioux uprising, a horrible, small war between the Sioux and area settlers caused by misunderstanding, greed, miscommunication, and mistrust. Many whites and Indians were killed, mainly because the starving Indians did not receive the supplies they should have from greedy and crooked government agents. Tory was one of the ten men killed when a group who went to rescue settlers were ambushed by Indians. He was the only one who survived through the night of thunderstorms, but died in the morning. Berte, pregnant with my great grandfather, and her two young children were among the two thousand settlers taken by covered wagons to Wisconsin. She later remarried, had more children, lived to be sixty-four, but perhaps could never recover from the terror she had lived through. Much later, my dad (Tory's great grandson) met Chief Little Crow's great grandson at a Kiwanis luncheon. They both apologized to each other for the terrible tragedy which should never have happened.

Sena, whose mother Kari was mentioned earlier, had an especially painful episode in her life. She was my grandmother Janette's mother-in-law, and Sena's past remained unknown to younger generations until after Janette died. When my mom and my aunt went through grandma's few belongings after her death, they found an old leather billfold of sorts. It was filled with papers which at first didn't reveal the heartache contained in them. The papers were pieces of a puzzle which when put together shed light on a new family secret. First, there was a page torn from the family Bible which listed the births and birth dates of all the children in Sena and husband Johannes' family. On June 22, 1865, there was in the Norwegian words "born to this world" daughter Randine. Wow! We had always been told that my grandpa, Sena's son Rudolph, was their oldest child, born in December 1866. Another paper was written by a parish priest who married Sena and Johannes on the same date that Randine was born. So now we know there was an illegitimate child who church records show was baptized, but died within a couple of days. When my parents, who by this time had this information, traveled to Norway, they learned from a cousin of my mom's that Sena would have had to endure the scorn and ridicule of fellow parishioners during her pregnancy. She

45

was made to stand in a sort of pillory before services, and church goers could decry her situation or spit on her or offer other indignities before they entered the church. What a display of (un)Christian love!

The last piece of the puzzle was a paper written and signed by a local official that attested to the couple's identity, listed their date of marriage, and "wished God would go with them as they travel to this foreign land." They left for America in August 1866, hoping to find a better life than they were leaving in Norway. Johannes was the youngest son of a large family, and as such had no inheritance rights in the Holmen farm. Primogeniture was widely practiced, with the entire farm passing to the eldest son, or daughter if she was the eldest. Johannes got the patent to his farm in Wisconsin in June of 1878, where he and Sena lived until they died. At his death, the farm passed to my grandfather Rudoph, their oldest son. Both Sena and Johannes became early founders and lifelong members of the small Lutheran church near the farm. I have found their graves in a nearby small cemetery and managed to read and translate the words on Sena's marker. It reads, "You will no longer see me here beneath this ceiling of stars, but rather find me in the great saints' garden living in God's day." Rest well. Maybe moving for me wasn't as tough as I thought.

July 4. On my early walk at the Shell Lake cabin I saw four jet streams so I know that Bob is here celebrating the holiday with the whole family. Before I left home yesterday, I put a bottle of calcium (used to treat cows for milk fever) in Bob's stainless steel vet bucket, and hung it and the beam hook to lift a cow in the garage. In case a vet call comes for him he'll be all ready to go. I shared in his career to a large degree, by putting him through veterinary school, being the bookkeeper in his first two-man practice, and always taking calls and knowing his farmers and a little about vet medicine. I shared Bob's dream. I miss him terribly, but can't imagine how he could possibly have managed to be having a life at this point wherever we would have lived. He

46

realized this sooner than the rest of us and was able to do something about it.

July 29. The Forsmans came today and took the bed that their daughter will use in her new home. That left a little extra space in the garage so I could rearrange things there better. Without a basement, the garage does double duty as a place for the car and storage. Yesterday I planted the hostas and anemone that I took from the yard in Barron. I dug up the Jack in the Pulpit plant also, transplanted it, and will hope that "he" can survive in his new home. As I watered the plants I thought of their getting rooted in a new spot, and that's what I'm doing here. Every day I feel more at home; I know I made a good call coming here. Bittersweet I will call this home, a fitting word to describe all of life. Missing Bob, as always.

Cousin Mary, having written <u>Max the Troll,</u> is so encouraging. She self-published her first book, a process so different today because of the internet options. Another note to self about writing a book: Just do it. But first I must start living a life, being a part of the larger community. I've put my physical life back together, better and faster than I hoped I could, so now I have to move on with living. I went to church a week ago at Bethel Lutheran Highlands. Another time I will try the service in the downtown Bethel Church to see what I think.

July 31. I must write about the lucky penny I found today. This is the one year anniversary of Bob's car accident; his first suicide attempt I now believe. I found the penny on Mississippi Street here, the name of the street I lived on in LaCrosse until I was five, the first home I have memories of. The penny is a 2014, shiny and brand new, like the brand new to me home in Hudson. I feel rooted here already after only one month, but I must get out of my own little world into the larger world. The last of my cardboard boxes are being sent out with the recycler today, a sign I've moved in!

August 7. Living my life has started, baby steps, and one at a time. I went to church at Bethel last night, a Wednesday

47

evening outdoor service, met the lady pastor who Lori knows, plus a few other people. I gave my phone number to the pastor who will give it to a parishioner who is involved as a volunteer in a hospice program. He called this morning, and I will contact the volunteer coordinator. I reread the Robert Frost poem, "The Road Not Taken", such a favorite of Bob's.

Two roads diverged in a yellow wood,

And sorry I could not travel both

And be one traveler, long I stood

And looked down one as far as I could

To where it bent in the undergrowth; ...

I shall be telling this with a sigh

Somewhere ages and ages hence:

Two roads diverged in a wood, and I --

I took the one less traveled by,

And that has made all the difference.

We certainly did follow the lesser traveled road, hopefully not leaving too big a footprint as we did. I miss Bob more as time goes by, perhaps the hardness of the last years of his life is fading from my memory. He like all of us was not perfect, but he was a good, good man. As one friend wrote on the sympathy card to me, "He made everyone he met a better person." I am thankful he knew how to relieve his suffering and was capable of doing it. Peace dear Bob.

August 8. My Hudson home is oriented the same way that our home in Barron was, my parents' home in Eau Claire, and the family cabin on Shell Lake. These houses face north, have south and east windows, but no western exposure. My dad chose the lots that their home and the cabin were built on and sited the houses as he thought best. I was only lucky in having the same sitings in Barron and Hudson. Thoughts of my dad made me wonder about his death; he, like Bob, died alone, both probably by choice since

my mom and I were almost always with each of our husbar
too was ready to go through the valley of the shadow c
fearing no evil. Both knew whose hands they were in. And dad,
like Bob, perhaps just let go. These two men, so important to me.
Both of them, I feel, are proud of me and how I'm going about life
alone.

August 13. It was two days ago that Robin Williams died
by suicide at age sixty-three. He had recently been diagnosed with
PD, perhaps he had been suffering from its symptoms for far longer.
Of course, the similarities to Bob were obvious and painful. Only
one month ago reporter Maggie Fox on NBC Health News told
about another reporter, Diane Rehm's experience with her husband
and his suicide. Diane told her, "His PD had become unbearable.
He just kept getting weaker. Knowing that his PD was going to get
worse rather than better, he said he wanted to die." Diane said he
was so brave...he did not want to carry on this way. "You have to
respect someone else's wishes...And he was finished with his life.
" 'I am looking forward to the next journey' he told me."

August 14. Bob communicates with me in the jet streams
he provides. Today, in the midst of all the publicity of Robin
William's death, his message couldn't have been clearer. Through
all the jet streams I saw today he's telling me that sometimes death
by suicide is not cowardly or selfish or wrong. Sometimes it is a
graceful, selfless way to end a wonderful life that has become
burdened with suffering. It is a person's way to take the first step
into the next life. Rest in peace.

August 28. Now the real business of care taking for mom
begins. She's been having dizzy spells, with no known cause. Her
pacemaker was replaced with no complications, but the dizziness
continues. Is this maybe more her feeling of loneliness or fear of
being alone? I know all too well from Bob how the mind tricks the
body into pseudo symptoms. He had progressed to the point of not
wanting me to be gone from home. That's what was tough for
me—where was my life in the care giving? This is why neither I

nor my brothers can agree to live with mom; how could we maintain a life of our own when she needs constant looking after?

My thoughts often return to this care giving dilemma; the care giver is not unaware of a person's dire straits, but he or she cannot let the person know this. To do that destroys whatever hope of a future the one being cared for has. Mom, like Bob, seems to look for verification from me of how debilitated she's become. By denying this in the hope of building her confidence, I can appear unsympathetic which isn't true. Mom has changed enough since Bob's death that now I cannot imagine how I could have handled both his and her care taking needs. Bob maybe knew the strain I was under, but I never heard him say that or in any way indicate it. As has been the case for several years, the antidote for me is being with children and grandchildren.

September 14. This week I've been following an interesting and enlightening TV series about the Roosevelts. A comment in regard to Teddy was, "the mark of a great mother is that she instills in her children a self-confidence that will benefit them all their lives." I would call this giving one's children their wings. My mom didn't give me my wings, but my dad certainly did, and Bob encouraged their further development. Hopefully he and I did the same for our sons.

September 15. A new experience for me this past weekend was attending my fiftieth class reunion. I graduated with about 450 other classmates so my connection to most of them was tenuous, if there at all. I had been able to dismiss invitations to other reunions with ease—why did I want to see those people I wondered? But this time I decided to attend the informal event and a small group get together for the few of us who attended a small, college linked grade school for many years. One of the biggest surprises was how old all these former classmates looked! That was said in jest of course, but it is one of the mysteries of "advanced" age that others my age appear so old, but it doesn't seem possible that I am as old, and no doubt look it also. The other surprise was how easy it was to erase fifty years of life with all its wear and tear, and find we were still friends. Maybe we have learned to act with grace, which my dictionary defines as: "Skill at avoiding the inept or clumsy course; a sense of fitness or propriety; mercy, clemency."

I planned to make the weekend one of both class reunion activities and time spent with mom. I stayed at her house Friday and Saturday nights, took her clothes shopping, to her church services, and out to eat. It's becoming imperative that we find other living arrangements for her even though she can't understand the need for it. I was awakened Saturday night to find her standing by my bed, clearly upset, saying she'd been looking all over for me, even in the garage, because she hadn't been able to find me. Even though she gets Meals on Wheels at noon, and we've hired women to come in to make her breakfast and supper and give her medication, she now needs twenty-four seven supervision. My brothers and I feel the weight of making such a decision for another person.

September 16. The jet streams were here again as John and Andy departed for Barron to attend the funeral of a good friend of ours who died suddenly of a heart attack while on vacation. Life is unpredictable; there are no guarantees, no promises made about when or how it will end. Bob often spoke of this way of dying as "what a way to go". When I was younger I couldn't agree with him on this, thinking that living in any condition was desirable. Now after seeing many friends, relatives, Bob and mom, suffer physical and mental hardship, I have come to agree with him. A sudden ending to a good life is perhaps "the way to go", but of course often not a choice we are able to make.

October 10. On my walk I wished Bob would appear as it had been days since I'd seen his jet stream. I looked to my left, and there he was, seemingly streaking through the sky immediately per my request. Later on there were several more streams shortly before I got a call from a woman at the Our House memory care facility in Eau Claire, letting me know there was a room available

51

for mom. She said there were other people interested so we had to make a decision that day. This was what my brothers and I had talked about in general terms, but the decision to accept or decline was one I wasn't going to make by myself. I called Pete who said we don't have a choice, we need to accept and move mom to a place where we can feel she is safe.

During my phone conversation with mom today I realized that she again confused me with her sister Glady. She maybe sort of remembered that Bob had died and said she supposed Pam would now want to find work of some kind. Oh, I have a job, a year and a half of trying to help give Bob a life and a year of the same for mom, and all the while trying to find a life for myself without him.

October 15. My sixty-eighth birthday, and I so wanted to see a jet stream as I left Eau Claire after celebrating at lunch with mom and brothers and sisters-in-law. Soon there was a beautiful one to the west, so Bob must have taken note of the date; he wasn't as good at remembering dates as some of us, and in good humor accepted any teasing about it. In the evening, I went to a small group Bible study, and when asked how my week had been I fell apart. All the people, members of the church I have only been part of for a few weeks, were so understanding and caring. Joining the church has been so positive for me, from lefse making for the food fest, to the new member meetings, to small group studies, and a monthly ladies' study group called "Circle". These women are all unconventional and full of life, and I'm one of the youngest, our oldest is 102 and mentally intact. Moving here to be near family, and belonging to a church, have provided as soft a landing after a move as anyone could ask for—thank you everyone for your support.

October 20. This was move in day for mom who seemed to be doing well with it all, helping pack her clothes, watching Dixie and me put her initials on them, deciding what she wanted in her overnight suitcase. Time will reveal whether the move now when she already has some dementia will be confusing to her. We wish she would have thought about and agreed to a move out of her home before she had dementia; I'll try to remember my thoughts on this issue when the time comes for me to perhaps make the same kind of move. Bob would have agreed that we siblings had to provide twenty-four-hour care for her, but living in this kind of setting was what he had so feared for himself for years. He saw both his mom and then his sister languish living in such circumstances, no longer able to care for themselves but sad and diminished by their physical and mental limitations. We left mom in the dining room in hopes that she will be well.

October 22. This evening I drove to Matt's house to see the three boys off on their trip to Nym Lake in Canada, site of the cabin Bob and his friends built in 1972. He had requested that some of his ashes be strewn over the land there, and they will carry out his wishes on the first anniversary of his death. They plan to find a spot whose direction references both Willmar, Bob's hometown, and Barron. They will find and plant three small white pines, his favorite tree, and strew ashes to insure their health and steady growth. How true that nothing is ever lost in this world—Bob's body will nourish the trees and the soil, and perhaps produce a stray mushroom or wildflower as well. There were jet streams heading north in the evening sky so Bob will arrive before they do.

October 27. Today there were the most glorious jet streams ever, streaking over the entire arc of the sky so I could be under them for much of my walk. As I felt Bob's presence, my thoughts turned toward eternity which is like a circle. A circle is forever and has no beginning and no ending; this describes our spiritual life. Our earthly or temporal life is a straight line touching two sides of a circle; we come from eternity and we go back to eternity at death.

My training to be a volunteer with Adoray Hospice, completed on October 21, was an in depth look at the meaning of life and suffering, compassion, death and grief. A quote I was particularly impacted by was one of William Blake. He said we're "spiritual beings given this physical life so that we can experience love." The teachings of Christianity bear this out; in the man Jesus, we see a human example of God's love. Our goal is to try to live in love to others as he did. My hope is that as a volunteer I can bring love and compassion to the people in hospice care and their families. I'm sure it will be an emotional journey with each new patient, but it is when we feel that we are our most human.

November 2. Today we celebrated All Saints' Day with a beautiful service at Bethel. Pastor John said, "death is not separation, rather it is a reuniting". Of course, he meant that when a person dies he or she is reunited with all who have died, the company of saints. What a concept, not a separation but rather a reuniting! We were invited to write the name of someone who has died on a leaf, then attach the leaf to the tree at the front of the church; written large on mine was Bob's name. Today or tomorrow will be the day that twenty-nine-year-old Brittany Maynard will take a lethal dose of drugs to end her life. She was diagnosed with terminal brain cancer and since then has become an advocate for "death with dignity". All of the callers to a local radio station spoke in support of her decision and for the right to die with dignity. Do I hear Bob talking also? I've been remembering the beloved pets he put to sleep when life had become burdensome for them, Penny, Mitts, Jake, Blue, Greta, and numerous others as a vet. Maybe I need to become a quiet advocate for the right to die. Two of my close friends, women my age and members of my Barron church, agree with me on this according to posts they made in regard to a Facebook story about a woman who died by doctor assisted suicide. One friend said, "I'm thinking it would have been much easier for you and your family this way. I still think of Bob often. He was such a good guy!" From the other friend, "This right would have made a huge difference for everyone in your family, especially Bob. There wasn't a nicer person." What loving support this gave me.

November 26. Mom's worsening dementia is a vortex threatening to suck me into it. Her delusions are her reality; I'm fighting hard not to let them become my reality. I stood at the brink of the abyss of depression and hopelessness with Bob, vowing every day that I would not fall into it. Since mom's condition overlapped Bob's worst days by such a short time, I shouldn't even try to imagine how I would have kept my head above water if both of them had been so in need of me at the same time. Occasionally though, I wonder, how could I have done that?

November 28. Long ago I wrote a poem about how we discern God; it's not with our brains or by scientific method, but rather through our hearts and our spirits. Often, He is revealed in the natural world of order and beauty and intricacy. One of the lines of the poem was, "when geese fly south in perfect V, my spirit helps my mind to see". Today there were those geese, flying south in a V, one after another becoming the leader so no one tired needlessly—how do they know when to leave, where to go, how to change leadership? Only because they are part of the order, the wonder, of the universe held together by God, or the Great Spirit, or the One, or whatever name we choose to call the Omnipotent.

December 13. Mom is no longer mom, but when her spitefulness is directed at me it's hard not to react. Thursday when I visited her, she honestly said that because she's suffering (I assumed because she has to live where she does), she wants her children to suffer. Later she said that while "everyone" talks about her wonderful children, they don't know the whole story. She is blaming us for moving her out of her home and into a memory care home. My brothers report not hearing this kind of talk from her, nor does anyone else. Often, I have noticed her negative feelings about women—her sister, me, some of her friends, an aunt she lived with long ago, her only granddaughter, sisters-in-law. At times we don't do what she wants or share her opinions which can be biased and strong. Mom and I are different in many ways, her world a narrow one with so many people who are "out to get her". Horizons can be widened by reading a variety of books which she never did. And her world was so filled with worry; her equation was that the more one worries about someone the more that shows love—I cannot buy that idea!

December 23. All the Omans, especially mom Jenna and dad John, are awaiting the birth of their first child. He or she is a bit overdue; perhaps he or she will be a Christmas baby. Today I visited with my hospice patient who is edging ever closer to death, now not eating or drinking. On one of my visits she gave me a gift so precious that I will treasure it forever. She has been mostly unresponsive during my visits when I sit quietly, sometimes reading or maybe rubbing her hands. I usually pray the Lord's prayer, and once when I finished, she opened her eyes and said, "I think an angel sent you to me." Hearing that made me realize how worthwhile my volunteering can be for the patients. Yet another instance of how much effect we have on other people, whether or not we're aware of it. I do not know who J.B. Miller is, but a quote of his or hers expresses this idea better than I can. "There have been meetings of only a moment which have left impressions for life...for eternity. No one can understand that mysterious thing we call 'influence'...yet every one of us continually exerts influence, either to heal, to bless, to leave marks of beauty; or to wound, to hurt, to poison, to stain other lives."

After visiting with one so close to death and while also awaiting the birth of my fifth grandchild, I thought of the similarities between dying and being born. My thoughts often turn into poems, mostly unwritten because I forget them by the time I have pen in hand. This one I remembered however, and it expressed this idea.

We live our span of years on earth, whether long or short, bound by time.

On each end we slip either from or to the eternal realm. Both are a birth of sorts,

maybe with pain or with a fight. But then the doors open wide, and we are born

56

either to the splendor of heaven's glory, or to the beauty of earth's fresh light.

God's blessings on both the dying and the unborn.

December 24. Another beautiful girl, Rose Julia, was born this morning, after much hard work on Jenna's part and lots of caring and concern from John. Alleluia, all is well! She widens the radius of our family and will be well loved and respected for who she is. Hospital workers told us we can bring food and presents and celebrate our Oman Christmas in one of the hospital conference rooms—this will be an unforgettable celebration!

January 13, 2015. Being able to take two steps away from mom's dementia is not as simple as I thought it would be; I must have been deluded by the fact that I don't live with her and see her perhaps only once or twice a week. Her phone calls and repeated pleas for me to take her home—does she mean her home, or to my home, or her childhood home—have to be ignored. My attempts to console her or pacify her fall on deaf ears. When Sarah listened to one of her phone messages, she said mom sounded much like Bob did in the last months, needy, dependent, childlike. Sarah's right, and as in Bob's case, there's nothing I can do to make life better for her. And that inability to help is construed by her as was by him as a lack of sympathy. But neither knew or can know the pain that their situations cause the helpless care giver. Her dementia, my lonesomeness for Bob and our life together, and all the changes I've gone through these past months at times make me feel as fragile as a glass ornament, ready to shatter into a thousand pieces. That's when I have to remember all I have to live for and have yet to enjoy, and the impact, small though it may be, that I hope to make in the lives of others. Usually I feel strong and solid, hard to break, and able to handle the hand I've been dealt. As the effects of Bob's last couple of years wear off, the stronger I get and the more I miss the man I loved so well. As Jane Hawking, wife of the famed Stephen Hawking, said in the movie "The Theory of

Everything", "I have loved him. I have done my best." And Bob loved me, I know that now and always knew it.

Late January. Sarah Noffke wrote, "A day will come when the story inside you will want to breathe on its own. That's when you'll start writing." Has the time come for all my stories to be written? I struggle with the idea that my story isn't any different than many that have been told. I've read books written by or about widows and how they've handled the death of their spouse. Books and stories about immigrants and their struggles are numerous. Literature, fact and fiction, about care givers and their patients abounds. My story about my twenty-seven-year battle with epilepsy is as of yet unwritten, but even that scenario was detailed in a book I read several years ago. I look for inspiration, or maybe the kick in the pants, to help me tell my story. Jack Canfield's quote helped, "If you can't find the book you're looking for, it must be you're supposed to write it." Or Maya Angelou makes writing almost mandatory by saying, "There is no agony like bearing an untold story inside of you." Ernest Hemingway told others to, "Write hard and clear about what hurts." And motivation comes from Janine Shepherd who said, "When we share our stories, what it does is it opens up our hearts for other people to share their stories. And it gives us the sense that we are not alone on this journey." I will continue to write.

What I last finished reading is Alice Munro's story "In Sight of the Lake", a tale told of a flashback memory of a woman suffering dementia. It touched nerves already way too raw because of mom's situation. A book in a similar vein on my reading list is Pauline Boss' Loving Someone Who Has Dementia which grapples with the perils of care giving someone who's "here but not here". This book underlines and puts an exclamation point on my life with Bob, even more a care taking burden than mom because I lived with him all the time. Dr. Boss ends her book with the thought that when dealing with someone with dementia—and I now believe Bob suffered from a form of it also—we have to be content with a good enough relationship. The sufferer is here but not here, and the loss

of the real person is ambiguous loss. We have to be content t<
in a gray world, perhaps a bit like Alice's wonderland where
nothing is as it seems. This is my calling now, to walk the journey
with mom as I did with Bob, and also to walk my own walk. Maybe
I have expected too much of myself the past three years filled with
the demands of Bob and mom, leaving so little chance for me to
nurture myself. There's been such a dearth of laughter and fun, so
much loss and sadness. I've been trying hard to make a life for
myself, one filled with more joy. It will not be the same life I had
however, as described by E. Kubler-Ross. "The reality is that you
will grieve forever. You will not 'get over' the loss of a loved one;
you will learn to live with it. You will heal and you will rebuild
yourself around the loss you have suffered. You will be whole
again but, you will never be the same. Nor should you be the same,
nor would you want to be."

January 29. In a TV show I watched last night, a character
was said to have had "his grandfather's heart". Hearing that I
wondered, whose heart do I have? Who will have my heart? What
is the legacy I will leave? Lately I've been thinking about these
questions. It's not obvious to me whose heart I have; does that
mean I'm a mixture of several personalities? Great grandmother
Sena, the one so spitefully treated because of her out of wedlock
pregnancy, often reminds me that I should not be judgmental of nor
mean spirited toward others. The thought has occurred to me that
one of my tasks on earth is to somehow right the wrong that was
done to her; that task is perhaps a "mission impossible", trying to
point out the nastiness of judging people. We should all assume
that everyone else is only trying to do his best at living a life.

Gleaned from what little written record was left about
Sena was the proof that she moved courageously past her young
life and hardships in Norway to make a life for herself and her
family in America. Her obituary said, "she was of a quiet nature,
always devoted to her home and family, where she will be greatly
missed." The poem in the newspaper write-up has three stanzas,
each starting and ending with "One less at home...One more in

heaven". And again and again I remember her tombstone inscription, blurred and mossy, about how she's now in the saints' great garden, such a lovely picture.

February 1. J.C. Watts' quote gives me more peace about Bob's end of life decision. He said, "It doesn't take a lot of strength to hold on. It takes a lot of strength to let go." So true for Bob, also for all of us parents who must sooner or later let go of our children, true for anyone who has tried to downsize and pare down possessions. We use so much energy trying to hold on to what we should easily let go of; perhaps the tendency to acquire rather than divest is in our genes. I have questioned whether it was strange that I could so easily give up my thirty-five-year-old life in Barron, my home, my friends, my church, small town living, all of it. Did I let go too fast only because I had a chance to sell my home, or was it truly time to leave? So far, I have not second-guessed myself; I haven't tried to reverse any of the decisions I've made for my new life. Today it was announced that Harper Lee will publish a second book, written long ago but not published. She is eighty-eight years old and still up for this new adventure, inspiration for me to "keep on keeping on".

February 5. John's thirty-sixth birthday; tempus fugit! A generation has passed since his birth, and now he's a father. I look to his daughter and my other four granddaughters, to him and my other two sons, to myself and my life, and backwards to my parents, grandparents, and all the others who preceded me and whose genetics I carry. As I glance around my bedroom, what I call my "family room", I see what a story the things there tell. I see the journey of my ancestors who left their lives, homes, and hearts in Norway, the trunk they would have packed with some of the things I've stored there, and furniture and items that were part of their lives in America. What's not revealed are the reasons they emigrated, the hardships they endured, and the kind of life they found in a new home. How easily I have always accepted my comfortable life made possible by the work of so many others.

February 10. I finished reading The Journal Keeper by Phyllis Theroux, impressed by how opposite was the course of our lives once we were single again. She married, had three children, and went through a heartbreaking divorce. She raised her children, and once they were grown she lived alone. I married, had three children, watched them grow up with my husband, and then spent a few retirement years with him before his death. At that point, sixty-seven years old, I had never lived alone. I went from living with my parents and brothers, to dorm life during college, to being married for forty-five years. Never in all those years had I lived alone. Always I had arranged my schedule around that of someone else, or at least I had tried to be mindful of the needs of those I was living with. Ms. Theroux found it exhilarating and comforting to form a loving relationship that led to marriage at age sixty-six, whereas I've found that having had a solid relationship for so long I have no need of another one now. There is a bittersweet element of being alone, a freedom to not have to take other people's schedules into consideration, freedom to stay up until midnight or eat supper at 7 pm, or just snack all evening, or watch a favorite TV show now or then. But the bittersweet part is when I get into bed without someone to snuggle with, when the car needs maintenance that I need to have done, or the shoveling won't get done unless I do it. Mostly though I'm content with this new life alone, knowing I've been so well loved for so long by one man, and still am by my children and their families, my mother, and my large extended family.

February 12. Today was the first time I led the Bible study in the small women's group that we call "Circle". The ladies responded well and talked easily. At the end I read the song "Will You Let Me Be Your Servant", meaningful to me and appropriate to the lesson on witnessing to our faith. By the end of the reading many of us were in tears. I've always been open to people and have become even more exposed and vulnerable since Bob died. This is good, and underlines what I've come to believe is one of my roles now, to be a gentle companion to others, to laugh, and cry, and share their journey.

February 18. I know for certain that while I don't want to leave this life any time soon, I'm ready to die. And I'm also ready to live and enjoy life to the fullest. That's the tension that exists for us—we should be ready to die but excited and able to live happily now. Knowing this about myself I realized once again the reason for Bob's death by suicide. He wasn't at all afraid to die, and indeed trusted God to take care of him in death. It was finding joy in this life that he could no longer do. Some people in his circumstances of a debilitating disease can find a reason to live, can pry open the nut to find the meat of a meaningful existence. He could not, probably partly because of the changes in his brain caused by PD. The cruelty of these effects of PD on him scarred him and me forever.

February 19. In my chapter three life I want to be a role model for my three daughters-in-law. Because I was so well loved by my mother-in-law, I want to live up to her standard. She was a warm and loving person who treated me as if I were her own daughter. Unlike me, she had a daughter, Bob's sister, who was beautiful and talented, another woman for me to emulate. Bob's mom was a gentle, kind grandmother as well, yet another way I can copy her.

February 24. Currently I'm reading Anna Quindlen's Lots of Candles Plenty of Cake. Anna is a bit younger contemporary of mine, and a product of the changes our baby boom generation saw and often brought about. Her voice is slightly more strident than mine, but much of what she writes resonates with me. She writes how we women "age into confidence, while men, losing power, status, and strength of youth, age out of it." Later she expands on her ideas about aging. "That's the hallmark of aging, too, that we learn to go deeper, in our friendships, in our family life, in our reflections on how we live and how we face the future. Equanimity in life equals going deeper into what has real meaning." You are so right Anna.

February 26. Life has so much fullness for me, in part because of all the meaning I find in everything. I wear clothes that belonged to someone else and feel their presence; I might be wrapped in the love of a grandma as I wear her apron, or feel stylish when I wear my artist aunt's sweater or scarf. I play another aunt's piano which she said she pounded out songs on after my uncle died of a massive heart attack, making her a widow at age fifty-nine. Bob's second wedding ring—the first one eaten by a cow after he took it off to work on her—hangs from a chain that I wear to assure me that I haven't lost him, I simply can't see him anymore. I look in the mirror in the morning and smile as I see my dad's smile reincarnated in mine. I hang art work by artists I know, I make food from recipes of loved ones, and use the furniture that came from family members or was found serendipitously by Bob or me.

February 27. There are many women, some of them famous and some I know, who count their mother as one of their best friends. There are others, several I know and love, who along with me cannot claim this. I'm of the opinion that the mother-daughter relationship is the hardest one to get right. My feeling has been that I'm not quite the kind of daughter my mom expected to have. Sigrid Undset, in her book Jenny, said, "No woman has ever given birth to the child she dreamed of." I should add that there's no doubt that she loves me, and I love her, but I wasn't the compliant little girl who would grow up to be content as only a Mrs. Somebody. My mom told me many times about the advice my sixth-grade teacher, a man with no children of his own, gave her and my dad at a conference. He said they would never have a problem encouraging me to read or do school work, but they should make sure that I knew how to cook, clean, and be a homemaker like most women in the Fifties were. I learned to cook and clean and take care of my younger brothers like my mom taught me. But I also loved to read, learn new things, play the piano and sing, knit, fish, walk, and water and cross country ski like my dad did (except knitting which his mother taught me).

My dad, who had two brothers and no sisters, hoped he would have a daughter. I was the first of my parents' four children, and the only girl. My dad always made certain that I knew he had confidence in me to become anyone I wanted to be. He had a wider view, embraced a bigger world, than my mom did. He was a Renaissance man with varied interests who never made me think there was anything I couldn't do because I was "only a girl". Mom would have defined my role; dad set no limits to what I could achieve. Near the end of her life, mom said, "You always were the special one for your dad." He spent Valentine's Day 1999 in a nursing home, rehabbing a hip injury from which he never fully recovered. As a gift to him, I wrote a poem which assured him that no matter how many other men there were in my life, he had been the first man, the one who gave me my wings.

February 28. This would have been Bob's sixty-ninth birthday, a day filled with memories of him. Matt, Janna, the girls and I went to visit mom in Eau Claire. Many times during the day I looked at the clear blue sky to see jet streams, Bob's reminder he's with us. When in Eau Claire I always stop by mom's house which is now vacant, but where mail is delivered. There was a flier from a local hospital; one article was about a three-step process which attempts to prevent people from committing suicide. The last step is to persuade a person considering suicide to take a different course of action and seek the help he or she needs. "One of the problems facing people who are considering suicide is that they don't think things will ever get better. So, it's important to help them realize there is hope, they will not feel this way forever, and things will be different." This couldn't be true for Bob. His future held no promise of ever being better physically or mentally; rather the specter of more deterioration and incapacity haunted him. His last big hope had been the DBS surgery which, despite its risks and unknown outcome, he was willing and eager to undergo. Even those of us who loved him and were close to him could not imagine how devastating for him was the loss of hope at its unsuccessful outcome. It did not give him the much-touted improved quality of life with PD.

March 1. I went to see the movie "Still Alice", the third in my movie trilogy which also included "The Theory of Everything" and "The Imitation Game". All three presented life situations which in some respects mirrored what Bob and I faced with his PD. Alice Howland suffered from dementia and cognitive impairment; Stephen Hawking continues to battle ALS; Alan Turing's life long struggle with depression and eventual suicide had never been highlighted until this movie. I left all three movies emotionally drained and questioning how we, and after Bob's death, only I coped with his PD's deteriorating effects.

My current bedside book is A Bittersweet Season by Jane Gross which recounts the years when she and her brother walked with their mother through the last years of her life in assisted living and later in a nursing home. Much of what she writes rings true to me in my current role as one of mom's care givers, watching her slip further into the tangled maze of dementia. Also, my current hospice volunteer patient is a ninety-six-year-old woman with Alzheimer's Disease. Today at the end of my visit she smiled and told me she was so glad I came. I hope that means I'm making it a bit easier for her as she takes her walk toward death. What's unbearable in the lives of those with dementia is not their death, but rather the loss of their essential self before they die.

March 2. A poem I love comes from a little book about rock cairns, those structures on paths that point the way or might be placed as a memorial. A nurse who we got to know when Bob had his DBS surgery shared our fascination with rocks and gave us the little book Rock People by Joel Carter as we left the hospital, full of hope on Good Friday, 2013. I reread the poems often, and my favorite speaks to the feeling I've had since moving to Hudson. The title is "Something Solid"

Falling into the

abyss is not such

a bad thing.

After plummeting

through the darkness you

eventually hit something solid.

That's when the door

opens and you finally

know you're home.

It seems fitting that the home I've chosen, Hudson, was the city where Bob and I spent our first married night in the Hudson House Motel. It is still here, in the same location as in June of 1968, looking much like it did then. Excited newlyweds that we were, we escaped our wedding reception as fast as we could, a move we later regretted considering we had many years together ahead of us. The memories of our first hours as Mr. and Mrs. have never faded. We checked into the motel and jumped into bed, both of us inexperienced virgins madly in love. After about an hour we realized we'd hardly eaten at the reception so we were hungry. We got dressed and ran across the busy highway, now an interstate freeway, to a little place called Grouchy Don's, long gone. We felt on top of the world and wondered if the few customers there on that Sunday evening could tell that we'd been married only a few hours before. We ate hamburgers and went back to the motel to spend our one night honeymoon. Now I call this beautiful city my home. It's nestled on the St. Croix River, a favorite of Bob's and on the border between Minnesota and Wisconsin (our two home states).

It's the first home I've chosen on my own—it is the something solid I hit after plummeting through the darkness.

March 3. This is the most excited about the coming of spring that I've been for many years. Last year's spring was so taken with sorting, packing, and moving that the season passed almost unnoticed, being only the time between winter and summer. I've been putting green everything-- decorations, pillows, candles, and glassware in my home, and am growing increasingly curious about what plants that I brought from the Barron yard have survived the move. Hopefully they will have put down roots so they can start to thrive in their new environment. It's impossible not to draw a parallel between them and to what I've done with my life over the past months, successfully I think.

March 9. This was a special day for me, affirming my belief that one of my purposes now is to connect with people and share my ideas about God and the meaning of life. Near the end of my walk I heard someone call my name from a stopped car. It was Skip, my choir director, who asked if I lived nearby to which I answered yes. He said he'd wanted to tell me how much he had appreciated what I said at a recent Bible study we both attended. My statement had been that the cross is a "way of living, not a way of dying." What I meant was that I see Christ's cross as a symbol of his endurance and of God's love in the face of human cruelty and evil. It is a victory over death and destruction, and a symbol of hope for us that we too can endure and overcome to find new life. What is expected of us is a life of service to others with Christ as our model, service and compassion to all, not only to those who are like us or ones we agree with. We too will stumble under the weight of the cross, but God is loving and has promised to be with us, so we too will endure.

Last night I finished reading <u>A Bittersweet Season</u>, finding in the ending the recounting of the death by voluntary starvation of the author's mother. This was yet another affirmation of Bob's death by suicide at the end of his walk with PD. A care taker who knew her mother said of her, "Enough is enough. She got tired of suffering. You do after a while. She still had her mind, and had decided." And the author said of her, "That was not the way she wanted to be remembered, as a human being transformed and wasted by illness...She was true to her proud character to the very end."

March 12. At Circle today, Betty said she thought I'd been sent here for a reason, leading me to wonder if that could be true. Maybe that reason is for me to carry on the kind of work that Bob had in his career with the animals. He brought healing to them and friendship to the farmers who owned them. After our retirements, we both volunteered at the schools and as BeFrienders, volunteers whose job is to listen non-judgmentally to those who need comfort and reassurance. The last months of Bob's life the emphasis was on him and his needs; neither of us had much chance to look outward, not even to our children and grandchildren. So now, in Bob's absence, perhaps I am to carry on alone trying to bring healing and friendship to others. It would be what Bob would approve of and encourage me to do.

March 16. Often, I think there's more to people, and objects, and situations than meets the eye; there are layers of meaning that we have to dig through to fully understand a person, or object, or situation. Stars, for instance, are far more than lights in the night sky. I was astounded to learn, probably from Bob, that in some cases a star's light comes from so far away that the star itself is no longer in existence. Wow, amazing! Soon I started thinking of those non-existent stars as people who have died. They are no longer with us on earth, but we can yet see their light. Shortly after Bob died I bought myself and my kids large, 3D cardboard stars, complete with tiny holes and a light bulb within which shines through the holes. I called them our "Bob lights" and we keep them in our windows.

No date on this but only a quote from Mark Weber's book Tell My Sons. "Most of us are in need of inspiration. ... We need those people to share their stories so we can draw inspiration from them for the living of our lives." So many writers have given me inspiration, have let me feel a bond with them, have shared feelings with which I can identify, have shown me a new way of looking at life. I owe them a huge debt of gratitude.

March 24. This morning I was as lonesome for Bob as I've ever been even though he gave me two perfect jet streams while on my walk. I saw the remake of the movie "Cinderella" yesterday, and was maybe still enraptured by the romance of the fairy tale. We had our own fairy tale moments—in truth years of them—now the memories for me to go over and over and cherish. So many other memories, and thoughts of the blessings that flood my life-- my children and grandchildren, friends old and new, a home of my choosing in a city of my choice, nature all around me, songs waiting to be played or sung—ah life, how full, how wonderful!

This kind of wonderful life was what Bob was being denied, or at the least his mind perceived as being denied, by his advanced PD. He was tired of fighting, of grabbing on to a new hope to find it wouldn't fix him. His tiredness and hopelessness were echoed by a character in an episode of "Grey's Anatomy" I recently watched. This man had excess fluid in his brain—the same problem as Bob's sister suffered—which mimicked Alzheimer's. He could have had an operation to drain the fluid, but it would have come back. He decided, amid his wife's tearful objections, against the operation. When the fluid would come back he would have been left "to rot in a nursing home. Our life is gone, we'll never get it back" he said to his wife. Words that poignantly echoed Bob's thoughts in his last years.

The chronic illness story is being played out in my mom's case. She has several medical problems which would seem to have caused her death years ago, but she lives on with her dementia. When she tells me how hard life is for her, I don't agree with her nor break down in tears to match hers. Rather I try to give her a bit

69

of confidence in her ability to carry on and enjoy life however she can. I try to be strong or "tough", the same way I acted with Bob. Again, I'm faced with the dilemma, that of trying to balance on the razor thin edge of not succumbing to the patient's hopelessness while not appearing to be cold and unsympathetic. I don't know that I am successful at times with mom nor was with Bob, at least not near the end when his PD had affected his emotional state, especially increasing his paranoia.

March 31. My thoughts today have revolved around faith and its opposite, not doubt, but certainty. That makes sense since faith is not being certain, but simply accepting a truth without proof. The idea that kept going around in my mind is that what we are often told is that "faith is a gift". It follows then that because God is loving, He would not give faith to one person and deny it to another one; how unloving and unfair that would be. My ah-ha moment today was that whatever faith a person has is his gift, given by God. Maybe that faith is only in the fact that two plus two equals four; maybe it is the faith that the sun will rise in the east and set in the west; maybe it is a person's wonder and awe at the intricacy and beauty of nature. Or perhaps faith is, as one of my sons has explained, the force that holds the world together against the natural tendency of it all to fall apart. Faith is how we can perceive God, influenced by our culture, the time in which we live, and our circumstances.

Having been raised by Christian parents, I had accepted the tenets of the church that they and my church leaders and teachers taught me. It wasn't until I was twelve that I first questioned some of those ideas. At that time these uncertainties unnerved me; I looked at what appeared to be perfect faith in others and envied it. This doubt scared me, kept me awake at night, and disturbed my peace of mind. My once secure faith took another hit when I was a freshman at Luther College. Yes, at a Lutheran school we were challenged to look at our personal faith, doubt it all, and find what we could accept as our own faith. This process of believing, doubting, and finding certainty has continued throughout my life. Now I have knit back together the yarns of my unraveled faith and made a strong fabric that is mine alone. The warp threads are God's love and his plan for salvation—a word from Latin meaning health—and the weft threads are what we weave in as we walk on our life's journey. My "Faith" poem expresses what I worked out for myself.

Come take a journey of faith with me

Worry not about what to pack.

All you need has been provided,

For God is loving and generous too.

The faith you're given will be enough.

Faith to believe, faith to doubt,

Faith to leap and know you'll be caught.

Faith to trust that you'll get where you're going,

Even when lost or unable to see.

April 6. Easter Monday, and what a huge discovery today when I looked at the area around my flagpole. There are at least ten groups of plants, in semi-circular form, outside the blocks around the pole. The plants look identical to what Bob called Trout Lilies, the kind of plant he looked for every spring in the ditch along Oak Street in Barron. They weren't the first plant to appear, but came up quite early in the spring. A couple of times, after a long, hard, winter, he was afraid they had died out. But always they appeared. He never thought of transplanting any, afraid they wouldn't grow in our yard in full sun. Early last spring, true to our tradition, without Bob I nevertheless walked along Oak Street until I found our Trout Lilies alive and well. Now, suddenly, here they are in my yard in Hudson, absent last year when I bought the house, but mysteriously appearing, vibrant and healthy, this year. You never cease to amaze me Bob!

April 8. Why are we given this life on earth? My favorite reason to date is that of Ram Das who said, "Really, in the end, we're all just walking each other home." What a marvelous picture of our calling for this life, acknowledging that we're only here temporarily, having come from, and are going to "home" however we choose to envision it. This is similar to William Blake's previously noted idea that we're alive so we can "bear the beams of love". He, like Ram Das, points to our responsibility and privilege to love each other, which, when we live in love, will ensure our own happiness. Hopefully our walking in love will inspire others in our lives to live the same way. Many experts are telling us that research shows that crucial to our health, happiness, and even longevity, is the strength of our relationships. "Love one another even as you love yourself." This should sound familiar, the rewording of the Golden Rule of "Do unto others as you would have them do unto you."

April 10. Today I had lunch with Nancy, one of the people who so inspires me. She's my age and continues to conduct choirs at a local college, her church, and a large group of young singers from second through twelfth grades. She said she has to "do" music, and the way she does it is by conducting. She could have had a professional career singing but opted out of that career path knowing that she would have had to "claw her way to the top" as she described it. Even in her conducting she doesn't want to push herself forward at the expense or discomfort of others. She said she tries to have her choirs rehearse to the point that they can't make a mistake—which she said is different than practicing to perfection. I had to ponder that for a while. Clearly music is her passion; I've never been as devoted to one particular interest or job, unless it would be to be a mother. I can echo Anna Quindlen's words in A Short Guide to a Happy Life. "I am a good mother to three children...I no longer consider myself the center of the universe. I show up. I listen. I try to laugh."

I have discovered a new "friend" in the history of women. She was one of the few Catholic women in the Middle Ages who is remembered. She said, "God keeps you. You are encircled by the arms of the mystery of God." Note to self to find out more about Saint Hildegard of Bingen.

April 16. What a wonderful gift I've received from Sarah's mom Anne, a lovely woman who grew up in England, has lived since her marriage near Pittsburgh, is also a widow, and an expert quilter. She contacted me several months after Bob died, asking if I would like her to make me a quilt out of seven of Bob's shirts. What an offer, how could I possibly refuse, except...oh, oh, the day before I had taken his useable cotton shirts to our local thrift store. I was so upset, but held out a tiny hope that I could retrieve them from the store. In a case of "it was meant to be", there they were, still in the back room about to be marked and put up for sale. Workers gladly gave them back to me, thrilled to hear how they'd be used. Anne made a visit to Sarah and Andy's home, partly to be able to give me the finished quilt. It is beautiful, a work of art, and incorporates every part of the seven shirts, pockets, labels, buttons, and all put together in different patterns front and back. It will warm me forever, and remind me of Bob whenever I look at it hanging on a comfortable chair in my living room. Thank you, Anne!

April 21. Recently one of my cousins suffered the breakup of a long-term relationship. There had been no promises made so there were none to break, but the suddenness of her partner's "I need my space" announcement jolted her. She wrote me that the kind of relationship she had always hoped to have would be like the one Bob and I shared. Her sentiment about us made me realize how somewhat unusual we no doubt were. We were true to each other, and only each other, our entire lives; neither of us had had a serious boyfriend or girlfriend prior to our meeting.

73

The words Pastor Steve spoke at Bob's funeral will make me quiver with emotion until the day I die. "Your love for each other, even in the middle of sickness and struggle has been a beautiful, Biblical kind of love that is patient and kind, and love that bears and believes and hopes and endures." Oh, our love wasn't perfect, none between humans can be. We could rub each other the wrong way, misinterpret what the other one said, and not be on the same page emotionally at times. This was especially true the last couple of years of Bob's life, affected as we both were by his advancing PD and the damage it was causing in his brain. But endure we did until the end.

April 23. Lately I've been thinking about how I used to occasionally feel empty, completely used up. I would tell Bob there was no water left in my well. He would say he hated to see me like that, unable to talk or do much of anything, certainly not able to be the inspiration that he needed to carry on. The mood would pass, maybe in a few hours or by the time I woke up the next morning. Now I can feel so full that I feel I'll explode. There's so much to absorb, savor, enjoy, digest—singing birds, a song in my head, thoughts of my family, the colors of nature, the houses I walk by, endless possibilities. Now I'm maybe an older version of my younger self, someone not as weighed down as I had been the last few years. I'm full but weightless; is this what joy can do to one? I try to figure this out—was Bob's condition so hard on me? Is that why he disliked seeing me so empty, so drained? Did he know I was suffering along with him?

Abigail Thomas, writer, mother of four and grandmother of twelve, said, "I love my grandchildren, not how they function (as do their parents) on a linear time." Hmmm, good observation. I look at each day vertically, morning to night, as many moments as possible filled with food for the body, the mind, or the soul. I worry less now about being productive, but strive more to fill my time with savoring experiences. A great afternoon might mean visiting with a friend over coffee, a satisfying evening can be one spent comfortably knitting with the TV on a favorite program. It's weird that as we age we have less time in the long run but more time in the short run. I have a better understanding of the saying that "the past is gone, and the future hasn't happened, but the present is a gift."

April 25. This year April 12 must have passed without my taking much notice of it. It was the day in 2000 my dad died from complications of his prostate cancer which had first appeared in 1979, then reappeared in 1998. He fell in January of 1999, injured but didn't break his hip, which helped hasten his decline. He described himself in his last months as "rusting from the inside out". He had been one of the most outgoing people I knew, usually with a big smile on his face, congenial and talkative. As his illness progressed he withdrew further and further into himself, visiting only with family and a few close friends. Following his death there were two divorces in the family, and while there were no children in either case, there was the pain of separation. Later, in the fall of 2004, my oldest brother was cutting trees at the family's lake cabin when he fell eighteen feet. By some miracle he lived, his brain intact, but was paralyzed from the waist down. His and my sister-in-law's adjustment and attitude have been exemplary, but they have had to walk through some dark valleys. One year later, in 2005, my middle son was married, a joyous occasion, but one marred only two weeks later when he found out that he had a severe mitral valve prolapse. Surgery to repair it was scheduled for January, following a surgery in November to repair a torn ligament. Knowing that our child's heart was stopped and in the hands of a surgical team was excruciating. The surgeon, one of the world's finest, was able to work his magic (we called it a miracle) and repair it. When twenty-nine-year-old Matt's young heart started beating again on its own, the surgical team cheered. We shed tears of joy at hearing this. Last in our string of losses starting with my dad's death was a growing recognition by Bob and those who knew him that all was not well. He had no sense of smell, a tremor in his left leg, softer speech, and less sense of balance. He diagnosed himself with Parkinson's Disease, so was saddened but not surprised when a neurologist confirmed the diagnosis in December of 2007. And with that, these past years of losses finally ended.

May 1. Spring has arrived it seems. Most of the plants that I brought from the Barron yard have survived not only the winter, but their move. Even the Jack in the Pulpit plant which Bob so lovingly tended after transplanting it from the woods is poking through the ground. Life is all around, the strength of it pushing new shoots out of the still cool earth, causing the trees to leaf out, and early flowers to bloom. We can't think that life resides only in humans, but in all of creation, plant and animal, bacteria, moss, and fungi. Our job is to tend it, manage it, help the struggling and encourage the thriving. Praise God for life wherever we find it!

Sometimes the tenacity of life is hard to explain. My mom, for instance, at nearly ninety-two, with high blood pressure, congestive heart failure, low thyroid, acid reflux, and impaired kidney function keeps on ticking. A way to describe her is a "life lived too long". Her dementia and paranoia are gradually increasing, both causing her increased anxiety. She says at times that she knows she's "losing her mind" (her words). One day she started to cry and said she didn't want to ask me the question she had, fearing that I would think she was crazy. I reassured her that she could ask me anything and I would answer. She wanted to know if my dad had died or was he alive. I had to tell her that he had died fifteen years ago, almost to the day. How could I lie and say otherwise?

One day she may say she's been visiting at a former neighbor's house; another day she may be fairly well oriented except she can't say which day, month, or year it is. She may say the workers at her memory care home don't have any idea how to cook, or do laundry, or help her. Two hours later she may say how good she has it where she is living. She becomes upset when she realizes she's misplaced the twenty dollars I left her, or look at her clothes and say she doesn't know where they've come from. She's been seeing little fires burning in the facility, refused to take a shower because there's lots of water on the floor, and thrown her purse and suitcase out a window she forced open. She worries a lot about her grown children, and sometimes thinks she should be cooking supper for us. But at times there's the almost audible sound of her sanity; she can barely hear it, would like to sing the song of sanity but can't remember the melody.

May 5. This was a day of small irritations, and the realization that while I handle the big issues of life and death, health and sickness, quite well, it's the little problems that upset and unsettle me. There's my lawn with its weeds and bare spots and the bothersome unknown creature who's eating plants, even the rhubarb. There's the issue of a magazine I subscribe to that was never delivered, the far too slow computer or internet, the dull ache in my back. Maybe I believe that I should be able to control these kinds of small problems, whereas often illness, or death, or job loss are beyond my control. Whatever the reason, I know I spend too much time and energy stewing about what doesn't matter. My life will be great even with some dandelions, without an issue of a magazine, with the ants that love to come indoors. And I may as well learn to coexist with whatever is eating my plants.

May 6. Tomorrow I will visit mom, and because Mother's Day is Sunday I will want to have a card for her with me. Picking a suitable card for her always poses a problem for me, trying to find one that expresses my feelings. We love each other as mother and daughter, and I'm well aware of all she has done for me, but many cards go way beyond expressing a simple "Happy Mother's Day". Some make mother seem like she's one's best friend, not true for our relationship. Mother may be portrayed as an important mentor or as the sweetest, gentlest person on earth, neither of which describe the mother I have. My mother was mother, a hard-working homemaker devoted to her family, and to making a home for her husband and children. She was a good mother in the only way she knew how to be, and I was a good daughter in the only way I knew how to be. Neither of us was the mother or the daughter the other envisioned., but we did our best at being each of them.

A small book I found years ago is titled <u>Will You Still Be My Daughter?</u> By Carol Lynn Pearson. It's one I should have shared with mom years ago, but regrettably never did. In this touching story, "mother" is an oak tree who drops an acorn and it roots and becomes her "daughter". Throughout the daughter's growing up, both of them realize that they are similar in some ways but different in other respects. When mother notices differences she asks, "Will you still be my daughter", to which daughter responds that she will. One of these questions is, "But if you sing a different song than I do, will you still be my daughter?" The answer, "And yes, mother, even though I sing a different song than you do, I will still be your daughter." And so poignantly for me, daughter asks, "But mother, if I did not grow to be just like you, are you disappointed?" The answer, so perfect, "Oh no, you are you, and you are better than I ever dreamed."

May 8. The story of Jack and Fern. In the last few days I noticed a plant coming up in the area where I had transplanted several from Barron. The hostas and coral bell had come up earlier, but in this one spot nothing had appeared. I had forgotten what else I might have brought and decided that whatever it was hadn't survived the move. Now I see that what's slowly emerging is a fern. The ferns on the west side of the Barron house were always the last plants to appear in the spring, providing the explanation for the late appearance of this one. The amazing fact about the Barron ferns is that they never appeared until after a propane gas tank was removed from the yard. It had sat on several cement blocks which we also took out. Then, with warmth and rain came the ferns, lots of them. Bob the scientist told me that the spores of those ferns could have been in the ground for hundreds of years, waiting for all the right conditions to emerge. Again, the amazing strength of life! And equally marvelous to me is my Jack in the Pulpit, another transplant. When Bob planted it in Barron he didn't give it much of chance of living. It beat the odds however, and not only survived but thrived. More tenacity. We need to remember this strength of life when we ponder death or the Easter message of resurrection. Whether this earthly body that we inhabit for a few years lives forever is not important. What is crucial is that we understand that we're part of the whole cycle of life, the messy, imperfect, wonderful life imagined and brought forth by a loving power we call God.

May 11. A recent episode of "Grey's Anatomy" revolved around the sudden death by car accident of Dr. Grey's husband Derrick. She had to be the one to order the removal of the life support system when he was declared brain dead, and I sat in tearful sympathy as she said her good-bye to him. When she came back to their home she said, "I would go back to the house, Derrick's and my house, and it didn't feel like home. I need to feel like I'm home." Maybe this same feeling was why I could leave Barron so easily. The house, the town, all of it was Bob's and mine. After he was gone it didn't feel the same, not like home. Carla said that it must have been hard to be there because we did things together, were with couples together, saw the same sights together, constant reminders of the fact that now it was only me.

Now for mom, more loss. She suffered another stroke, or maybe two, and the medical team's approach going forward is to not do therapy. I read between the lines on her discharge papers to her memory care home and clearly, given her previous stroke, her age, her dementia, and other underlying conditions, the goal is to maintain her new "normal". It would be questionable that any progress could be made with rehab, and the move now to yet another facility for rehab could be devastating for her already fragile quality of life. When we brought her back to her memory care home she seemed glad to be back to what is now at least somewhat familiar and homey. There were her two favorite chairs and her clothes and friendly care givers saying, "welcome back

Julie". She even soon told me I might as well be on my way home—that's a rare occurrence!

May 14. The continuing plot in "Grey's Anatomy" in which Dr. Meredith Grey suddenly became a widow gave me more to think about. She was told that her light had gone out, and later heard that she needed a safe harbor, a place where could fall apart. The harshness of our life during Bob's last few months nearly extinguished my light, and we knew that his light was gone as well. Two of us with little ability to shine because of PD. And perhaps both of us were suffering because neither of us had a safe place in which we could fall apart. We couldn't light the other one's light nor fill each others' empty well because we were depleted; all our energy went to live our daily lives. We could accomplish little else in a day except eat, keep the house in order, take a short walk, and maybe have one short outing, often for one appointment or another for Bob.

With Bob, and now with mom, I have to keep fighting the idea that I can give anyone else a life. Other than the act of birthing my three boys, I, like everyone else, can't put life on a plate and hand it to another person. Sometimes when the boys were young, I tried to make life perfect for them; I tried to make Bob's life better during our years together; for those fighting alcoholism I occasionally tried to help smooth the rough spots. Now mom is the one who looks to me to help make her life better, but there's little I can do to change anything for her. Yet I struggle not to feel guilty about this, knowing that each person must find his or her own happiness and well-being.

May 19. This is one of those times when I'm so lonesome for Bob, especially the physical Bob. When I look at his picture or see someone who looks like him, I can almost feel his hand on my shoulder or his body snuggled next to mine in bed. We were good snugglers, often spending most of the night curled into each others' curve. Yet, maybe surprisingly, I in no way want to find a replacement for Bob. I long for him, for the Bob before PD took over his body and then his mind. It's at times like this that I must give myself the speech that says I was blessed to have had nearly forty-eight years with him, first dating and then married for forty-five. That same voice in my head tells me to remind my kids and their spouses to treasure the good times together—there are never enough of them.

Last week I took my annual trip south of Eau Claire to the cemeteries where the grandparents, great grandparents, and other relatives are buried. What a beautiful drive on a blue sky May day. The cemeteries are King's Valley, Lewis, Upper Church and Lower Church, now Peace Lutheran Church in Pigeon Falls. All are so lovely, set in the rolling newly green hills which must have reminded those Norwegian immigrants of their home in Norway. By the time I stood in the last one, I was overcome with emotion. Before I left the cemetery, I walked into the limestone church next to it. Built in 1948, it replaced an older church on the same land and is two years younger than I am. As a child, I often walked the few steps from my grandparents' home next door to the church. The door was always unlocked so I could walk in and soak up the peacefulness I found inside. The church has that effect on me even now, calming me and connecting me to my roots. The end of my visit was a stop at my dad's cousin's home nearby. I so enjoy being with her, and others in the family if they're available, letting her fill me with coffee, cookies, and love.

May 26. This weekend provided one of the biggest ah-ha moments of my life. At sixty-eight years old I have learned that within the circle of family love, we are safe to express our opinions even if they differ from those of someone else. We can have disagreements and yet love each other and be friends. Such a simple idea, but one not well taught in my family of father, mother, and four siblings. Because we feared conflict, we rarely learned how to handle it. Some always agreed with the prevailing feeling to keep peace at any price, or others might have buried the conflict deep inside only to have it explode volcano-like later. Neither way is healthy, and in the long run paves the way for disaster.

A takeaway idea from the series about the Roosevelts was that "Teddy could outrun his depression, but because of his physical limitations FDR could not." Was that true for Bob, that in the end he couldn't outrun his depression? It had been a monkey on his back since youth, the cause unknown but probably partly because of his dad's alcoholism. He never seemed to be able to feel completely comfortable in his own skin, which for me has never been the case. Did this uncomfortableness bother him? We never talked about it, but my guess is that it did. Then, in his last months, bereft of hope of getting better even after having DBS surgery, the black cloud that had always hovered nearby increasingly blocked the sunshine of his life. He denied being depressed, a couple of visits with a psychiatrist didn't diagnose it, and being on Prozac proved ineffective, taking away both the lows and the infrequent highs he might have felt.

June 1. I'm rereading Dan Brown's Inferno because it's going to be made into a movie, much of it set in Florence, Italy where two of my cousins live. This passage stood out for me: "...the worst kind of loneliness in the world is the isolation that comes from being misunderstood. It can make people lose their grasp on reality." Is this perhaps what Bob felt much of the time, especially near the end when his brain chemistry was so altered by PD? Whether or not he actually was misunderstood, he often perceived that he was. His friends and family loved him and forgave him his shortcomings, but he didn't always believe that. In the end I think he only trusted God to understand him, making it easier for him to put himself in God's hands.

Both Bob and my dad, neither of them perfect of course, placed a high priority on fairness. They wanted to be fair to the people they did business with, to the friends they knew, and especially to their children and grandchildren. My dad once confided to me, amid tears of emotion, that one of the hardest parts of being a parent was trying to be fair to his children while allowing for their individual differences. If one of us children received a gift, we all did, and that applied to grandchildren as well. My dad and Bob both shared, and realized, their dreams of having a lake cabin to enjoy with family and friends. Now with both of them gone, we all have to work together to share and maintain these places in fairness to everyone.

Every morning when I look in the mirror to put in my eye drops, I see my dad's smile, his eyes, albeit mine are brown to his blue, and his white wave of hair. I believe I never mourned the loss of my dad in 2000 because I carry him within me. I share many of his interests and traits, evidenced by the fact that even as a young girl it was with him I wanted to share my time. I have his curiosity for the world, nature, music, and so much more. He and I were most likely to be on the same wavelength, and my brothers more often on one with my mom. Having three sons I can easily understand the strong bond between mother and son. I don't know what kind of mother I would have been to a daughter, but I hope to always be a good mother-in-law to daughters-in-law, and a loving grandma to my granddaughters.

June 7. What a wonderful thought—the most important word in the Bible is WITH! This is what theologian Samuel Wells has said. We see this in passages such as: "The Lord be with you, and also with you." "Lo, I am with you always, even to the close of the age." God is not doing things for us, but rather is always there with us to comfort and to guide. Similarly, while the simplest course of action might be for us to do something for another person, we should only be concerned about being there with them. That's a bit risky, and means we have to open ourselves to the hurts and needs of others. Learning how to be with those at the end of life is at the heart of the training I took to be a hospice volunteer, and is the most important part of what I do as a volunteer. We call it being a "quiet presence".

June 12. Perception, the bane of human relationships and communication. If I say A, and someone else thinks I've said B, I may not be able to change his mind. I can explain myself forever, but the perception that I said B may persist. While it's fruitless to argue that two plus two equals anything but four, so it might also be fruitless to argue against perception. Errors of communication can sometimes be talked out, but talking and even actions may not be enough to change perception. On the world stage, incorrect perception can start wars and topple leaders, and on a smaller scale can ruin families and alienate friends.

June 14. Today I saw Marv; he's looking well after his recent months of heart problems, procedures to alleviate them, and the promise to go to cardiac rehab for the rest of his life. We talked for a short time about his experience, and soon he wanted to share how he looks at life differently now. He said what he's lost is his fear of death, and what he's gained is a new appreciation for life and the joy it brings. I said I shared his feelings about life and death, I and many other people I know. Whether it's our old middle age, or our Baby Boom mentality, or the openness we enjoy, we're talking about our mortality. Will we be cremated or buried; will we be spending all of our money or leaving something behind; will we have our mental faculties to the end? And everyone I've talked with believes God will be taking care of us after death. Although we don't know what the "afterlife" will be like, we accept the uncertainty the thought of it presents.

June 19. Whenever I see a person who appears to have PD—stooped posture, masked facial expression, slowed movements—I realize the well of emotion that I held back when Bob was alive. I may cry, or be nauseated, or shake as I feel pity for the person. These reactions, these emotions, were what I never showed to Bob. I felt the same way about the effects of his PD, although the daily exposure to him numbed me somewhat. But never, never did I let him see my pity, my visceral emotion evoked by his condition. I had lots of practice in hiding my pity. There was son John, born without a right forearm who never thought of himself as disabled. There was Dixie who had colon cancer at age thirty-five; she told me as I stood crying at her bedside after surgery that I had to be strong in front of her. Son Andy endured bullying by classmates but never looked for pity, only our support. Vern, whose fall left him paralyzed, counted on the family for support but never pity. Matt, suddenly in need of open heart surgery shortly after he was married, laughed and joked his way through recovery keeping us laughing so we couldn't cry. Through my twenty-seven years of epilepsy I tried not to ask for pity but only understanding of this often misunderstood condition. I love the slogan "pity, it's curable" --it's true!

June 20. Maybe I'm nearing the end of planting things at my Hudson home, but there's always the possibility of adding more. I've wanted these outside plants to tell a story much like most of what's inside my home. I've brought some plants from the Barron yard, taken some from the yard of the home in Eau Claire where I grew up, brought a few from the woods across the street from the cabin at the lake, gotten cuttings and plants from my three daughters-in-law, and of course bought some from nurseries. I keep questioning, will they survive, and more importantly, thrive? Much of the answer is in the transplanting. Did I take enough of the roots so they can establish themselves? Will my soil be right? Will they get enough sun, or shade, or rain, or too much of any of these? Aren't all of us like the plants, transplants put on earth? Why do some of us thrive and others don't? Do some of us adapt better than others, or are the thrivers only lucky to have landed in the right environment for them? Are the thrivers able to get their sun and rain and shade from those they love? So many questions, so much to think about as I plant, delphiniums here, an anemone there, then hope, always hope that they will survive and thrive.

June 26. Today's visit with mom brought with it the constant tug and pull of pitying her but not showing it. I adamantly hold to the idea that if even once I give in and show pity, I will destroy the front I put on to try to make her feel better. I tell her how strong she is and how well she's doing. We talked about missing our husbands, my loss much newer than hers, but how we have to be brave in facing our lonesomeness. Is this being callous? No, I think it's the approach that attempts to bolster mom rather than diminish her with pity.

July 6. This was the Fourth of July weekend, one spent with family at the lake and not soon forgotten. We had a fun day on the third, but because of stormy weather at night couldn't enjoy the town's fireworks by boat. Not a big loss as we watched from the dock. The Fourth dawned bright, beautiful, and warm, so by late morning all the little ones were playing in the lake. In what all the parents called a normally harmless activity, Elsa jumped off the anchored pontoon boat into the water. Sadly, in so doing she caught her right-hand pinky finger on a sharp hinge, which as she jumped, amputated her finger. Suddenly everyone was in action, all of us grown-ups wanting to know what happened, what needed to be done, could we find the finger for possible reattachment. Most important was getting Elsa, Sarah, and Andy into the car and on their way to the hospital in town. From there they were referred to a surgeon who worked in a hospital in the Twin Cities.

The short version of the story is that the surgeon recommended further amputation of the knuckle and an angle cut of the hand which made the loss of the little finger almost unnoticeable. Reattachment he felt would have little chance of success and even less chance that the finger would be usable. Elsa was released from the hospital that evening, going home so everyone could get much needed rest. Elsa was such a strong seven-year-old through all the trauma, and mom and dad were examples of calmness and courage in the face of a tough situation. So were the rest of us who witnessed the accident, especially Matt who had to find the finger, and the kids who didn't let this accident interfere with their love of their lake activities. As we left Sarah and Andy's home after visiting on the fifth, I said, "This is one more case in which we must hang together or we fall apart." That's always the choice we have to make.

July 14. Among my random thoughts lately is the one that I will gladly accept being this tiny dot in time and space as my life. I've known the love of my parents, and the confidence my dad gave me to face whatever life has brought. I shared a love with Bob so deep that I will always feel his physical presence, react as a giddy young woman whenever I see a Bob look alike, and find his messages to me in the jet streams and his voice in my head. While I could probably have followed any career path I would have taken, I chose to be first and most importantly a wife, mother, and grandmother, always my dream. My three sons and their families are my great love and source of strength. I've led three lives, a first one of preparation, a second one of homemaking, child rearing, and career, and now one of fulfillment. Strangely for me, this third chapter is a female dominated one. Growing up with three younger brothers and two male cousins, and then as the mother of three sons, my world was male dominated. The balance of people in my life has changed by 180 degrees, partly by the death of my dad and Bob, and also by the addition of three daughters-in-law and five granddaughters. Now in my single life I'm freer to cultivate and nurture female friendships. I have met many women through church, extended families, and community, and have more opportunities to be with them. This third chapter, like the first two, is being lived out in a world so wonderful, filled with love, and laughter, and learning. Of course, there's sorrow and challenges, but only so much as to shine a spotlight on the good. Thank you, God, or Spirit Over All, or The One.

July 20. Can I get through the process of selling and divesting my parents' home of over sixty years? This is not a surface process only, but rather like excising skin cancer when the doctor has to dig deeper and deeper. My brothers and I aren't only deciding what small pieces of our parents' lives we want to keep or sell; we're revealing character traits about ourselves and baring feelings we maybe haven't been consciously aware of before. I

87

have to question if, as the oldest, I have been bossy without wanting to be, and if so, not realizing it. Can the emotions which surface be the result of small hurts buried for so long? Can the coddling, or favoring, or smothering of one or another be showing up in feelings now being expressed? Maybe there's one or more of us who's trying for the first time to make sense of the rest of us as we dance around the edges of our emotions. We four would be a psychiatrist's dream these days, but for me, I'm thrilled to have the oil painting of the Norwegian church of my ancestors on my wall, and the three watches of two grandfathers and a great grandfather in the hands of my sons.

July 28. As I walked today I was thinking about the woman who is buying my parents' house—yes, it did sell, very easily to a couple who enjoy the mid-century look that it still bears. The wife is a university professor probably about forty years old, with no children. I thought how pleased my dad would be with her as a buyer, the one to take over his dream home so well built sixty-two years ago. Dad would have been my biggest supporter if I had chosen such a professional life. But, when I came of age in the sixties, there were typically far fewer occupational opportunities for women. Also, I dreamed of being a wife and mother in addition to any job I would have. Young women at the end of the sixties stood at the cusp of the era when women could do it all, have a career and be a mother and homemaker. Most American women of my mother's generation didn't try to combine the roles, and women of my generation were only beginning to work and parent. Common as a woman's having dual roles is now, juggling the two is not easy. In her beautiful book Gifts from the Sea, Anne Morrow Lindbergh wrote about her admiration for the young women who both work and mother. I see the struggle my three daughters-in-law have, yet recognize what an amazing job they are doing of being wife, mother, and career woman. The only advantage we have over men in this respect is that our brains are organized and fed with hormones to make growing, bearing, nursing, and caring for children natural.

July 31. Nancy recommended a book by Pat Conroy, <u>Beach Music</u>, in which I found more inspiration to write. "I have learned that a story untold could be the one that kills you." If this is true, it is the reason that all of us need to tell our story, whether we write it or not. I see more clearly than ever that the bottled up or untold perceptions of someone can poison a once solid relationship or undermine an entire family. Whatever hurts, real or imagined, that one feels, if left untold will almost certainly come out in a destructive, negative way. I've always been so afraid of conflict, even mild differences of opinion, but am trying to learn that meeting troubles head on is the only way to avoid greater ones in the future. Love is strong and can safely hold together those with a wide range of ideas and feelings.

Some of the people I know and love lead lives consumed by regret, guilt, paranoia, and grudges of past hurts. Thoughts of "If only I would have", "I should have", "He's got it in for me", "She always got what she wanted" fill the hearts and minds of many. It's better to live so that we don't have regrets later, won't be shackled by fear of others' intentions, or diminished because we can't let go of the hurts once felt. I've tried, not always successfully, to be open to other people and sympathetic to their unique personalities and problems, trying to believe everyone is doing the best job he can in his life walk. When son John was taking a grad school class about those with disabilities, he interviewed me about my years with epilepsy. It became the basis of his final paper which dealt with the challenges my seizures posed for me. One of his conclusions was that having epilepsy for many years sensitized me to others who had disabilities, made it easier for me to "walk in their moccasins", and respond to their needs. John could identify with this as he was my son born without his right forearm.

Much of chapter two of my life was lived in the shadow of my epilepsy. It was yet another of the brain disorders or diseases that have appeared in Bob's and my families in addition to his PD. Several of us have been migraine headache sufferers; my dad and now a brother had or have Myasthenia Gravis, a condition caused by a lack of the brain chemical acetylcholine which helps control muscle movement and coordination. My cousin's wife has M.S. which is a deterioration of the myelin sheath insulator of some nerves. My aunt had and died from Alzheimer's Disease, and now there's speculation that my mom, her sister, is in the early stages of it as well. Several people in both of our families have had strokes of varying severity, most recently my mom. Alcoholism, which is now considered a brain disease, has affected more people than anything else in the families.

Because I haven't experienced a seizure since July of 2004, my twenty-seven years as an epileptic seem to have been in someone else's life. For many years I have wanted to tell the story of this part of my life to help others understand epilepsy, and by understanding it, to fear it less and more easily accept those afflicted with it. It is one of those "invisible" conditions, not noticeable on the outside of a person, like depression or addiction. Life seemed to get in the way of the telling however—raising children to adulthood, homemaking, and jobs outside the home. By the time I retired from my full-time job at a bank, Bob had been diagnosed with PD and we were first time grandparents.

The day in early February 1977, began like any other day with getting breakfast for Bob and sons Andy and Matt, four and one. We had settled into a comfortable routine after arriving in Rice Lake only a few months earlier. Bob had taken a rather roundabout way of becoming a veterinarian, but was now fully enjoying his work. I liked small town living; both of us were sure this would be a good place in which to raise the boys. I couldn't have been happier in my role as full time homemaker and mother, having been up to this time either going to school or working to put Bob through school. This was a period characterized by lack of stress, as everyone in both families was healthy, income was steady and sufficient, and I was finally living the life I'd always dreamed of.

On this Saturday afternoon, my parents had come for a short visit, about an hour's drive from their home in Eau Claire. I was glad to see them but had been having some strange sensations in the late morning. Even though I have an advanced degree in English, I couldn't find words to describe these feelings to myself or anyone else. It wasn't nausea, or pain, or discomfort, not deja vu thoughts—just odd, and never before felt sensations. Suddenly, soon after my folks had come, my brain "blinked", and I fell down. I got up immediately, but of course my mom and dad noticed what had happened.

They were concerned and wondered if I was OK. I answered that yes, I was fine and had no idea what could have made me do that. My dad asked if I was pregnant, but my mom quickly responded that no, that wasn't possible, I had only recently quit nursing Matt. They asked that I see a doctor as soon as possible, to which I promised I would, mostly to assure them. I was sure this incident must have been due to my fluctuating hormones and my body trying to adjust to its non-pregnant, non-nursing state. A couple of weeks later I did consult with a doctor. He dismissed the episode as probably nothing to be concerned about given that I was a healthy thirty-year-old. Was this the end of the story?

Having two young sons and a veterinarian husband with a hefty on-call schedule of every other night and weekend, I fell into a pattern of attending to their needs and not paying much attention to my own. We met new friends in the neighborhood, the community, and the church we joined. One neighbor, in particular, seventy-three-year-old Selma, was a favorite. She loved to have the boys at her house and always treated them to cookies or other goodies. I relied on her for advice, recipes, and the warm, grandmotherly hugs she so freely gave us.

Weeks and even months evaporated rapidly, spring then summer followed the February incident. I noticed with increasing frequency that I would wake up and experience a sensation much like those on that February day. They were fleeting moments that left no tell-tale signs of having happened. Because no one else was either awake or around to see me at such times, I doubted the reality of what I felt.

However, soon I could discern a rhythm to the "spells" as I now called these odd moments. They were clustered around the times of my menstrual period or the two weeks before it when ovulation occurred. Having had migraine headaches since I was thirteen, I knew from reading about them that these two times of the month were when estrogen levels drastically rose and then fell. I attributed the spells to the effects of estrogen and adopted a wait-and-see attitude. So far, I felt I could take these brief spells in stride and deal with them later if they worsened. Nevertheless, usually hidden, but decidedly there, was the gnawing fear that something in my brain wasn't right.

Most of the time I told Bob that I'd had a spell or two, but it was several months before he saw me experience one. When he did, he told me that I suddenly stopped talking and my eyes got a faraway look in them. As he witnessed more of the spells, he related that I also smacked my lips or made chewing movements. Eventually other family members who knew me well noticed my spells, whereas casual acquaintances weren't able to detect any change in my behavior. Having medical training, albeit with animals, Bob was frustrated by the puzzle the spells presented. Thinking maybe there would be an answer in a blood analysis, he collected a blood sample and sent it to an animal laboratory. Rather than call the sample human blood, he labeled it "rhesus monkey", an animal who not surprisingly has a blood composition very similar to that of a human. The results were disappointing in that they showed only a slight shortage of calcium, nothing which could explain the reason for the spells.

One day while visiting with a friend who was a nurse, I had one of my typical spells. She was curious about the event and listened as I gave her details about these spells. She said, "You don't suppose these are seizures?" I felt a chill run through me at the mention of the word seizure, but quickly dismissed the idea as hard to believe. I, like most people, thought of seizures as only being of the grand mal type in which a person loses consciousness, swallows the tongue, flails about, and needs time to recover afterward. I had once seen a boy have such a seizure while at a Bible camp. He shook violently, turned white, almost fell in the lake, and had to go to the medical building with the camp nurse. The memory of that terrible episode has never left me; I still get an uneasy feeling when I think of it. It was this memory that caused such dread when I heard the word seizure. Nothing more about my spell was said that day, and I hid the horrible word far back in my mind.

Andy and Matt were the fulfillment of my lifelong dream to be a mother, and at this time I was lucky to be a stay-at-home mom. I helped at the Vet clinic once in a while and did the bookkeeping and billing as well. After renting a house for over a year, Bob and I started looking for one to buy. Our searching was unproductive, probably because this was a small town with few houses for sale. Then we heard about a local contractor who built modest sized homes with a price tag to match. We decided to hire him to build us a house, found a lot in the newly developed north end of town, and signed the papers for an FmHA loan. The building went quickly, and soon there was plenty of work for me—finishing woodwork, painting walls, picking carpet, vinyl, counter tops, and cupboards, and then the process of moving out of the rented house and in to the new house. Homeowners at last, at thirty-one years old with two kids—about time!

Building and moving must have been distracting enough that I neglected to take the little impromptu survey that I had intended to take. I was going to ask people, "Two kids, or three, what would you say?" I was going to get a consensus for us to consider in our family planning, but before I did (and it no doubt wouldn't have been our decision maker anyway), I discovered I was pregnant with number three.

This was exciting news for the family, making for lots of speculation about whether it would be a boy or a girl. The odds seemed to favor another boy as I had three younger brothers, and my dad was from a family of three boys and no girls. During the first two or three months of my pregnancy, I had my spells about the time of the month when I would have had a period. Then, wonder of wonders, the spells stopped happening. It was fascinating to wonder if now that progesterone levels were so high, the estrogen couldn't have its way and produce any spells. The other two pregnancies had been relatively easy for me, and this one was the same. The absence of spells made life even more wonderful than before the pregnancy. I hoped that maybe there would be no more of them—ever, but always that small worry that they'd return.

On an early February day, 1979, baby boy Oman, John, was born, another easy birth, rewarding Bob and me with a cute, healthy baby. We brought him home to his two brothers who were anxious to meet their new playmate; well, not quite a playmate yet. I nursed all three boys, and John benefited from then current guidelines to breast feed for about a year. His last nursing was bittersweet for me knowing that he was our last child. Bob and I had agreed that after John's birth I would have a tubal ligation as our future method of birth control; three children seemed to be enough to nurture and provide for.

After nine months of being pregnant and twelve of nursing, I was looking forward to having my body back to myself. Naturally I was hoping the spells had gone the way of the dinosaurs, never to return. Soon after I stopped nursing, my first period returned, and then another one, for the first time in my life on a regular twenty-one-day cycle, a welcome change from my formerly irregular cycles. And so far, no spells, nothing out of the ordinary.

"Oh God, no, please no," I thought about four months after John's birth, "that couldn't have been a spell." But it was, followed by another one the next morning, then more a couple of weeks later until the old, dreaded routine began again. Never crossing my mind were any safety issues such as, "What if I drop John, what if I have a spell when he's in the bathtub?"; no one else in the family raised any concerns either. I had already brought Matt safely from infant to toddler; why should I not be able to do so for John? He was a good baby, the easiest of the three boys, but as Bob and I said, maybe that was because we had finally had enough practice as parents to be relaxed about it.

Life returned to its normal pre-pregnancy pattern except now there was another child to take care of. These were the days when dads typically didn't do as much of the day-to-day care giving for children as they do now. Also, Bob's busy work schedule didn't give him much freedom to do so on a regular basis. He was, however, terrific at playing with his boys, some catch in the backyard, bike rides, fishing outings, sliding or building snowmen in the winter. Bob had decided early in his life that if he were a father he would be the best one he could be. His own dad was an alcoholic, a talented, outgoing, loving man, but plagued with an addiction that meant he could be unreliable. Many were the times that Bob's family had made plans that couldn't be followed through because his dad was drinking. To a child, that loss of certainty in a parent can be devastating.

While Bob was a great father and excellent veterinarian, his working relationship with his veterinary partner got rockier and rockier. His partner had always practiced alone, and while he really needed someone to share the work load, he wasn't good at giving up control of the practice. After about three years of Bob's work in Rice Lake, his boss said abruptly one day, "I think we ought to call it quits." Bob called me to give me the news, turning my little world upside down. This felt like a script from a soap opera—the wonderful life I'd always dreamed of suddenly threatened. Making it worse was the fact that I couldn't do anything to change the situation.

Bob's search for another job started immediately. He and I wanted another setting as close to what we had in Rice Lake as possible, but this time Bob was hoping to find a somewhat larger group in which to practice so the call schedule wouldn't be so demanding. The job offer that eventually appeared was one that my grandma would have said was "meant to be". A three-man practice eleven miles from Rice Lake was looking for a fourth partner. The eleven-mile distance was key since Bob's contract with his current boss said he couldn't in the future practice within ten miles of Rice Lake should their relationship end.

What followed Bob's acceptance of the job offer were busy months of selling our house, finding one to buy in the new city of Barron, painting and staining in the new house there—our second new one in two years—then finally packing and unpacking, none of it easy with three youngsters in tow. Barron was smaller than Rice Lake, about three thousand people, but big enough to provide basic services and even have a fire siren that sounded at noon each day. Hearing the noon siren sound had been a treat for me as a young girl when visiting my aunt, uncle, and cousin who lived in a small town south of Eau Claire. I had fantasized about living in a similar small town when I grew up, and now found out that once in a while dreams do come true.

The nightmarish side of my life was the presence of what we continued to call spells. They were becoming more numerous than before and were now easily recognized by anyone who witnessed one. I'm naturally gregarious and talkative so most noticeable was my suddenly stopping my speech, often mid-sentence. In his role as "doctor" Bob, and I wanted answers to what was causing the spells, and we were frustrated in our not being able to find out. I described them to one doctor at a routine visit, but he

96

shrugged them off saying his wife was a stay-at-home mom like me and had strange thoughts too. What kind of medical training would have responded like that? Another doctor, a good friend of ours and a thorough doctor, thought perhaps the spells were a result of a burst of epinephrine, a good guess but it didn't lead anywhere.

As the months went by, I kept mental notes of when the spells occurred, and as before my last pregnancy they were always when I was having my period or ovulating. I coupled this with information gleaned from a doctor who was on the radio talking about premenstrual syndrome, or PMS. I put the bits and pieces together and decided, as I had previously suspected, that estrogen was somehow at the root of the problem.

A clear pattern, a medical background, awareness that the spells were real, and an inquisitive mind were what brought Bob to the conclusion that what I was experiencing were seizures. Again, that word—SEIZURE—nearly terrorized me. But I too had to acknowledge that it was a possible diagnosis. Bob thought I should set up an appointment to have an EEG, a test that could detect seizure activity, at our local hospital. Without telling me, he knew there could be serious underlying reasons for seizures, a brain tumor the most obvious. I scheduled the EEG and tried hard to stay awake the night before so I would be able to fall asleep during the test, necessary to its accuracy. I arrived at the hospital, nervous and sleepy, had the electrodes glued all over my head, got as comfortable as possible in a hospital bed, and did fall asleep for a few minutes of the procedure. After the test, I came home to wait for the doctor's call with the results.

He called the next morning with the chilling words: "They found unusual activity in the right temporal lobe which indicates you're having seizures originating from that area. We'd like you to come in tomorrow, Saturday, for a CAT scan of your brain."

"Thank you" was all I could say, and was then transferred to an appointment desk to set up the scan. Bob, the boys, and I were planning to go to my folks' lake cabin that night, which we did do as it was only about a half hour trip. We left the boys with my folks the next morning and traveled back to Barron to the clinic. Since at that time the CAT scan was a mobile one, there was a radiologist on board who could immediately read the results. The blessed news was that there was nothing abnormal about my brain nor the vessels in my head. We went back to the cabin and were met with tears of joy and hugs at the news. Seizures, yes, reason for them, no answer.

That night, lying in bed with Bob at the cabin, I felt the weight of the burden of information given me. For the first time, I thought about the word "epilepsy" and realized that I was an "epileptic". In words I could barely choke out, I asked Bob what he thought of me now that I had been diagnosed. "You are still you," he said, "nothing about my love for you or who you are has changed." Bob held me tightly but gently, and as he did, my crying subsided, and at last I fell asleep.

From then on however, my attitude toward my now named seizures was drastically different. Gone was my openness about them and my almost glib acceptance of them as some unusual, but harmless trick played by my body. In fact, I no longer wanted to talk about my problem or to be told by anyone who saw me have a seizure that I had experienced one. It was disconcerting enough to have these "epigastric sensations" as one source termed the feeling before the seizure, and then the seizure itself which I didn't remember.

Originating in the right temporal lobe, my seizures were the most common type of them, vastly different from the grand mal ones that most people think of in relation to epilepsy. A temporal lobe seizure can be as minimal as smelling a non-existent odor or hearing a non-existent sound. I never lost consciousness, but rather experienced "altered consciousness" during the seizures. Not until I'd had seizures for many years did I lose my balance, act abnormally, or do anything else that would put me in danger. They were for a long time more of an annoyance than anything else except that they were apparent to anyone who saw me have one. While they were quite predictable as to time of the month, their frequency was variable. I could have a few a month or maybe six or seven on a bad day.

Once I was diagnosed with epilepsy, my primary doctor referred me to a neurologist for an evaluation and treatment. Neither Bob nor I had any experience with specialists nor any preconceived ideas about what a neurologist would be like. I found out later that, similar to any profession, there are good neurologists and poor ones. Unfortunately, the one I was scheduled to see in the Barron clinic had no bedside manner. Even though I explained that I'd had seizures for nine years and had been coping with them very well, he wrote a prescription for Dilantin, a commonly used anti-seizure mediation.

Always somewhat skittish about taking medication, I asked him to explain possible side effects. Oh, none that you could understand he answered condescendingly, definitely none that could be worse than having seizures. My inquiry about whether my seizures, well documented as to their timing, could be related to my hormones brought another rebuff from the doctor. "I've never heard of any connection." End of visit.

After the visit I felt like all the wind had been knocked out of me. I filled the prescription however, and started taking the medicine that day. When the bright red rash appeared within days, first on my face and then spreading to the rest of my body—a rather common side effect of the drug—I felt vindicated. I wanted to ask the doctor if he thought I couldn't understand a rash. I called the doctor's nurse who told me to stop taking Dilantin and prescribed another commonly used anti-convulsant, Tegretol.

This was summer time, a beautiful one in Wisconsin, not too hot nor too cool, but one filled with sun shiny days to be enjoyed. Bob, the boys, and I rode bike, swam, visited the cabin, watched the boys' softball games, and picnicked. This was all fun and routine summertime activity, as routine as my seizures continued to be even though I was now medicated. Every time I had a period or was ovulating I had seizures, as always, the number was variable. Bob and I weren't surprised; nothing about my hormones had changed, why should the seizures?

Obviously the Tegretol wasn't alleviating my seizures. I reported this at my next visit to the neurologist who then added Depakote to my medication routine. Again, he wouldn't talk about side effects, and made no request for me to come in for periodic liver enzyme tests. I was told to come in for blood tests that would determine the titre, or level, of medicine in my blood. Many medications must show a high enough level in a person's blood to be considered effective. Each time I was tested, the titre was too low, so more medicine was added to my daily dosage, eventually reaching the point of seven pills, three of one drug and four of another, taken several times daily.

That amount of medicine soon started causing negative side effects for me. My energy level was going down, which for me was very unusual. My thoughts were foggy, I felt sleepy, and Bob noticed that by late evening I would sit with a blank look on my face and saliva running out of my mouth. My appetite waned, and at meal time I had to tell myself to eat something. Within a few weeks, Bob said I had to go to the clinic for a liver function test, in later years a requirement for anyone taking this drug. The test results showed highly elevated liver enzymes, a sign of possible liver failure. This was a Friday, and I was told to come back Monday for further testing.

Knowing how awful I felt and how important a liver is, I couldn't help but wonder what damage the drugs had already done. I cleaned the house, picked up the dog's droppings in our yard, planned out some menus for the family, and planted daffodil bulbs that would come up in the spring even if I weren't around by then.

I visited with my former neighbor Selma, my friend and substitute for my grandmas who were now deceased.

Monday's tests showed further worsening of my liver function, so our doctor ordered Bob to take me immediately to a hospital in Eau Claire. A moment that neither of us could forget was when Bob looked over at me in the passenger seat and said, "What have we done?" I was admitted to the internal medicine floor, given a physical, and taken off all medication. That night, jaundiced, weak, and aware of how serious my situation was, I faced my death. I was a month away from turning forty, but had been able to earn a college degree, marry the love of my life, earn a master's degree while he was doing the same, be the mother of three young sons, work to put Bob through veterinary medicine school, and help establish us in a small community where life was good. If I had to die, at least I was at peace with what I had accomplished and all the people I had been able to love and share my life with.

But wait, by morning my enzymes had miraculously already started to return to normal. The early prognosis was that my liver would recover and be fine if I didn't take the medicine which had to be metabolized by the liver; mine was allergic to it. I stayed in the hospital for two more days and returned home with a head clearer than it had been for weeks, and having lost about fifteen pounds since starting the medication.

Before I was discharged from the hospital, the neurologist who I now called "the doctor from hell", came to my room and said now we'd try another medication. My answer was an unequivocal NO because all anti-seizure medications at that time had to be processed by the liver. Again, I had been justified in asking him about possible side effects. He threatened to have my driver's license revoked and predicted other horrible outcomes, but I was adamant that I would not again compromise my liver with medication that probably wouldn't control the seizures which I had successfully lived with for close to ten years.

The fact that the seizures could not be altered by available medicines forced me to once again accept them as an unchangeable part of my life. The continued predictability of their timing convinced both Bob and me of their link to the fluctuating levels of estrogen. We were certain of this, but were unable to convince anyone in the medical community who we had contact with. This was at least as frustrating for Bob as for me, his being an animal doctor whose job was to identify the medical problem and then cure it.

Bob was certain that we could find a doctor who would want to delve into my case and produce an answer, or at least gain information about seizures from my case. He set up an appointment with an endocrinologist, a friendly woman who said it appeared that we knew more about my condition than she did; she wouldn't even charge me for the visit. I consulted a gynecologist who thought it would be helpful to take estrogen in the hope that it would even out my fluctuating levels. That was a terrible mistake as it produced a month's worth of many seizures. One of the days that month was my folks' fiftieth wedding anniversary party. I was helping serve lunch and visit with people, but it was rough in between the multiple seizures I had that day. At wit's end, Bob scheduled me for a work-up at Mayo Clinic in Rochester, convinced that I would get to see several specialists who would finally solve the puzzle. But, as soon as the word seizure was used, I was directed to see only a neurologist. He wanted me to come back to have an MRI which he thought would pinpoint an affected area, or focus, in my brain. I was understandably afraid of what the specialist would tell me the MRI had found. He looked me in the eye and said, "There's nothing abnormal about the results." Tears of relief, but again not an answer as to cause.

The older I got and the closer to the start of menopause, the more unpredictable the timing of the seizures. This was because as my periods were no longer on a regular cycle neither were the fluctuations in estrogen levels. On any given day I could have one, two, eight or more seizures, almost anywhere and at any time. People at my work place knew about them and were understanding of them, as was my family, especially Bob and our sons. This was my new normal, and had been for nearly twenty years until that day in August 1996.

Bob and the boys had left for Canada on Friday, a work day for me, but Saturday was my chance to go to Eau Claire and hang out with family there. My folks were at the cabin so I thought I'd have some fun with Paul and Carla and their young sons. It was about eleven am when I left Barron, coffee mug in hand, excited to be on my own with no responsibilities. I remember seeing the wayside rest stop on the east side of Highway 53, and then crash. I had gone off the road to the east, hitting a tree at probably highway speed. I crawled out of the car, noticing my broken glasses, smashed windshield, cut knee, and sore chest, no doubt from the seat belt I'd been wearing. Within minutes a car stopped, and the two people who got out said they were EMTs who always carried a body board. They called 911 and put me on the board against my wishes, but they were insistent.

The ambulance took me to an Eau Claire hospital, and after some much-needed cleaning up and a few stitches, I was released to Paul and Carla. I knew for certain that now Bob and the rest of the family would tell me I could no longer drive. There wasn't much of an investigation into the accident since it was a single car one, and there was no collision insurance on son Matt's old car that I was driving. This was the end of the story legally, but not for me, who at not quite fifty years old could not drive. Thankfully I was a walker who lived in a small town where everything I needed, including my work place, was within about a mile of home. However, without public transportation out of Barron, I was stuck there unless someone else drove for me. My plight didn't generate much pity, but I've never been quick to pity others; it doesn't seem to be helpful for anyone, myself included, to be pitied.

The accident, another bump in the road for us, in August, and then in November, the report that Bob had prostate cancer at age fifty. He never considered any option except to have the prostate removed in a surgery in Eau Claire on December 13, 1996. The cancer was thankfully contained within the gland so no further treatment was needed. The new nerve sparing technique left Bob with fairly minor functional problems which resolved within months.

With both of us past the rough spots, we headed toward John's high school graduation in 1997, and with it the prospect of an empty nest in the fall. John went to the University of Minnesota where Matt was a senior and eventually Andy would get his MBA. For a brief time, they all played on the same intramural hockey team at the U of M. We adjusted to life without sons living at home, and were lucky to see them fairly often. We always believed that our job as parents was to give the boys roots and wings, and then let them fly on their own. We also strongly encouraged them to remain close friends throughout life, in spite of differences of opinion or of personality traits. It wasn't easy to keep our mouths shut with young adult children—and we made our mistakes—but we tried to let them make their own decisions and to take the responsibility for their actions.

During these menopausal years, the duration of my seizures and actions during some of them worsened. There were the times Bob was called to come pick me up, once at the grocery store when shopping, once at a friend's new house I had stopped by, and once at City Hall where I had gone to pay a bill. While recovering from one seizure, my co-worker told me that I had sat down on the steps and taken my shoes and socks off. Crossing a busy street never caused a problem, but each time I looked left and right and then crossed, I wondered what would happen if I had a seizure at that moment. Perhaps the only time I was in danger when having a seizure was when some of us had gone out on the pontoon boat at the lake and were jumping in to swim and cool off. Bob saw me jump off, then soon realized I wasn't resurfacing. He was able to see my hair in the water, dove in to grab it, and pulled me into the boat. John was there, and for a few seconds was afraid I'd drowned. But I emerged without having swallowed water or having suffered any other injury.

Our early empty nest years were filled with changes, first my dad's death from his recurrent prostate cancer April 12, 2000. Bob semi-retired from veterinary practice that summer, a change I thought premature at the time, but later understood how physically challenging veterinary work with large animals, mostly cows, was for him; maybe PD was already weakening him. Matt earned a master's degree in engineering, and John graduated from the U of M; all three sons had good jobs and were successfully on their own. Bob retained his pre-semi-retirement call schedule, and I continued my bookkeeping work at a local bank.

By the summer of 2004 I was fifty-seven, and about ten years into my menopausal years. It was in July that my ovaries must have been giving up the last of their spurts of estrogen, causing a slew of seizures, odd sensations, and noises. On July 17, I asked my sister-in-law Dixie to take me to the ER at the Barron hospital as I was afraid that something was seriously wrong. Bob and some of the rest of the family were at the cabin in Canada, and Dixie and I were staying with my mom at the family lake cabin. All the tests they did that evening were negative so I was pronounced healthy. Nevertheless, knowing my seizure history, the ER doctor recommended that I start taking a new anti-seizure medication. Given my near-death experience with prior meds, I was hesitant, but by this time there were options that were not metabolized in the liver. The doctor assured me that Keppra was cleared by the kidneys so I should have no problems with it. OK, I said, rather desperate, I'll try it. From that day on, I never had another seizure, but as Bob and I reasoned, not because of the Keppra, but because my estrogen would never again rise enough to lower my seizure thresh hold to the point of having a seizure. End of this story, and while it would have been so gratifying to gloat about our correctness as to cause, there was no doctor who had believed us previously so wouldn't accept the answer now.

Today, at least in some circles, there is wide acceptance of estrogen-caused seizures. In an Epilepsy Talk feature called "Hormone Imbalances and Seizures in Women", dated August 11, 2013, I found my proof. What follows is some actual quotation and some paraphrasing on my part.

"Many women have asked doctors about the connection between seizures and hormones, but not every woman has seen her concerns given the attention she'd hoped for. There are scientifically documented connections between seizures and hormones that not all physicians are educated about. Hormones are chemical substances formed in organs and glands that travel through the body and bloodstream. They control muscle growth, heart rate, hunger, the menstrual cycle, and other functions. There's a dynamic relationship between hormones, brain function, and seizures. The brain regulates the release of the major sex hormones, estrogen, progesterone, and testosterone. These hormones can influence how the brain works. Estrogen has been shown to increase seizure activity, while progesterone can have anti-seizure effects. Seizures that are most likely to be affected by hormonal changes are partial seizures that involve the temporal or frontal lobes of the brain. These areas of the brain are closely connected to the hypothalamus and pituitary glands of the brain, which control the release of hormones. Levels of estrogen and progesterone in the body can affect seizures. Hormones may alter seizure thresh hold. Many women see changes in the number and pattern of seizures around the time of ovulation or just before and during the menstrual period. This is called catamenial epilepsy." Amen and thank you!

Back to 2004. It took several months for me to grasp that I was truly seizure free. Since a trigger for seizures can be stress, the biggest test of my new-found freedom from them occurred on September 25. Bob was on call that weekend so was not able to attend the concert in Barron that my cousin and his wife were coming to attend with me. Around 4 pm my cousin's wife called to say they wouldn't be coming as my brother had fallen from a scaffold while cutting trees on the lake cabin property. This was the accident mentioned earlier that left Vern paralyzed from the waist down. Never once during his extensive recovery, surgeries, and rehab, did I experience a seizure. So far, we were giving some credit to the Keppra, but we decided years later I probably wouldn't have had any in its absence. Not willing to risk my good fortune of seizure free years, I continued on the medication, slowly tapering off, until June of 2012. An important bonus of being seizure free was my being able to resume driving. After seven months of no seizures, Bob let me drive to visit John at his new home in Hudson. When I arrived, I asked him to get in the car, and we took a victory lap around his block, music blaring, tears rolling down both our faces, pure joy in being alive and well.

August 8. A TV show last night had a bizarre new idea for me to consider. One of the characters being investigated was found to have written random words on every wall in his house, a condition the medical examiner called "hypergraphia". As the word indicates, it describes someone who writes obsessively, and is often a symptom of temporal lobe epilepsy. Wow, that's the type of epilepsy I lived with for twenty-seven years. I looked up the word in a Google search, and in a WebMD site there was the description of hypergraphia. The information suggested that several famous and prolific writers had temporal lobe epilepsy. Is this why I often find myself doodling words on paper, blackboards, or in the sand? This could be the explanation for my doodling, but I know I'll never be a prolific writer, my only goal to finish this story.

There hasn't been much time to write this week however, the week in which we sign the papers selling my parents' house. I've asked myself a few times if I should be doing something so crazy as selling and cleaning out their house only little more than a year after selling my own home of thirty-five years and moving to a new one. But as Power of Attorney for my mom, I have to take the lead if we're going to do this. The time seems right as we know mom will never be able to return to the house, and sitting uninhabited isn't wise. Last year I was trying to incorporate Bob's life into my own, and make sure my sons were preserving his legacy in their lives. Now my brothers and I are sorting through our parents' things, far more valuable because of their meaning than their material worth. Throughout the process I've again tried to preserve a legacy, yet not overload myself with more stuff which can truly and so easily be a burden.

August 11. It is finished, cleaning out mom's house. In a process that will have lasted four months, my brothers and I, under Jane's guidance, have chosen what each of us or our children wants. We had the house appraised, then listed, and after a few showings received an offer the next day. We watched as the auctioneer and his crew removed all the salable items, and then spent a day carting garbage to the dumpster in the driveway. So, for me, two households' worth of goods accumulated over many years, sorted through—maybe now what remains in my care is manageable!

August 18. Last night I finished reading Go Set a Watchman, Harper Lee's newly discovered first novel. For me the most important idea came at the very end of the story, the one Atticus conveyed to Scout that your friends don't need you when they're right, but rather when they're wrong. I have never thought of this concept, probably because I avoid conflict and want everyone in my life to be at peace with each other. I can understand the truth of friends needing a friend when they're wrong; however, the Catch 22 here is that right and wrong are often a matter of opinion or perception, neither of which can be proven. This means we have to stick with each other in the face of differing opinions and accept that even though we may not agree on everything, we can be friends. Certainly, this must apply in families as well, a concept I am only now beginning to trust. When people truly love and respect each other, they can disagree, and in fact enjoy each person's differences and the strength of each one's ideas. Did I really have to get this old for this to sink in?

August 25. Yesterday the final chapter of the house on MacArthur book was written. The auction of mom's household goods, the orphan ones not chosen by the family, were sold along with those of another couple. It was very windy and cool, more like late September than August, but better than too hot and sunny. I thought I would be emotionally unfazed by it, but no, every so often my heart strings were pulled by one memory or another. The piano, with its original ten-year warranty dated January 7, 1955 in the bench, was delivered to our house on a bitterly cold winter night. I was eight and started taking piano lessons soon after we got it. My folks didn't play the piano, so clearly, they bought it in hopes children would use it. The auctioneer had a hard time getting a first bid, finally starting at ten dollars. An old man who knew it had been mine bid it up so that it eventually went for sixty dollars to someone else. The woman who bought it lived down the street, was a music teacher who had been teaching students with her electric keyboard for years. She was thrilled to get it and promised to take good care of it.

There have been other family auctions that I've attended—my dad's parents, my mom's farm long after her parents had moved away but still containing their things, my aunt's home, and my mom's aunt's home. Going to any household auction was a pastime of mine for a few years when my boys were young and I'd haul them along on a Saturday. Rarely have I been to a sale when I've not been struck by the meaninglessness of most things once the owner no longer needs them. It might be linens hand embroidered or crocheted, tools so well loved and used, artwork chosen with care, furniture gracing homes for generations—all often going for a few dollars or less. The lesson I took away is that we should live only with what is meaningful to us or useful in our lives. Otherwise, stuff is only stuff which can become the quicksand of one's existence, keeping one mired down in the unnecessary.

Now my parents' children and grandchildren or the cabin at the lake have a few of the things they held dear. Mom herself now lives in her memory care home with two rockers, a washstand that the TV she can't remember how to use sits on, and a little three drawer cupboard in addition to the bed and dresser that are provided. She has only what's useful because her dementia rules out her giving meaning to objects. People are important to her however, family and friends she's loved and cared for whether they're living or not. Look to those at the end of life to see what we should treasure—the answer is people, only people.

August 27. Lonesomeness can pounce on me as suddenly as a cat hunting a mouse. A smell, a picture, music, or maybe nothing can bring it on. It's usually Bob I miss, or my dad, an aunt, my boys when they were young. After I've wiped my eyes and gotten rid of the lump in my throat, I always, yes always, tell myself that I can't be sad that it's over but rather be glad that it was. I've been so blessed by the people in my life, especially my dad and Bob who are both gone but who gave me my wings and encouraged me to fly. My sons all chose wives who are strong women, and I have no doubt that they will raise their daughters to be confident, and comfortable in their own skin like I am lucky to be.

September 1. Today was one of those days when life is so full, of beauty, love, things to do, people to connect with. I could easily say I've had the chance to do and to have all I would ever want in life. In one of her books, Anne Lamott quotes the poem inscribed on the tombstone of Raymond Carver who died at age fifty. It is:

And did you get what

you wanted from this life, even so?

I did.

And what did you want?

110

To call myself beloved, to feel myself

beloved on the earth.

I can only agree with him, and say Amen.

September 2. I talked to Shirley today, wife of a man with PD. What pain, heartache, and struggle she bears as she deals with her husband who now is in a nursing home. He is angry with her for "putting" him there, but she could no longer care for him at home. Few of those in our PD support group are doing well or are even alive. What a terrible disease PD is.

But on the other side of life, it is the first day of day care for little granddaughter Rose, the first day of kindergarten for granddaughter Sofia, and soon for Svea, and Elsa already starting second grade. How quickly they grow up, but our job always, to help them do just that, grow up. Tears of sadness and of joy—God be with them all.

September 12. I am nearing the end of Wendell Berry's Hannah Coulter, a book Nancy recommended as one of her favorites. I think he wrote the ending of my book for me, an ending so fitting there is no way I can improve it. Hannah, a recent widow, muses about her life without her husband. "I was changed by Nathan's death, because I had to be. Our life together here was over. It was my life alone that had to go on. The strand had slackened. I had begun my half-a-life you have when you have a whole life that you can only remember. ...We were each others' chance to live in the room of love where we could be known well enough to be spared. We were each others' gift." Surely that was what Bob and I were to each other, a gift wrapped in love, now a memory which sustains me, guides me, and keeps me from falling into a pit of depression. For death is only the temporary separation of the living from those who have died. This gift is alive in my memory of it.

September 14. At a recent small group discussion, most of the people there felt that we don't like to talk about death. A couple of them said their adult children won't even let them bring up the subject, shoving it aside with phrases like "we don't have to think about that for a long time." But there was a minority of us who have become more comfortable with the reality of death, more accepting of it as the beginning of the next phase of our life, or a continuation of life in some other form, or the culmination of this life. And I believe that children, so often shielded from death, should be part of the inner circle of grieving when a relative or family friend dies. Three of my young granddaughters who remember Bob, especially the oldest who was five when he died, feel sadness at his loss, but say they "have him in their heart". On the one hand, I'm doing everything I can to hopefully keep me alive and well for many years; on the other hand, I don't fear death. I agree with those who say we can't fully live until we accept that we will die.

September 16. We're told that age has its advantages and disadvantages. A memory not as sharp as when we're young is one of the latter. Yesterday I saw the movie "Mr. Holmes", a film about what life might have been like for a ninety-three-year-old Sherlock Holmes. Throughout the movie he tried to remember the ending of the last case he worked on more than thirty years previously. He struggled with the knowledge that his memory was failing rapidly, he who once relied so heavily on it for his work and his idea of self. In the end, he reconciled himself to his new normal, living life so as not to need the sharp memory he once had. Similarly, these past days I've been trying to find what I can still do and what activities are now out of my zone of possibility. One afternoon I took out my violin, tuned it, and tried to play a song. While I can remember the few basics I once learned, I soon discovered that my body—neck and back and arthritic fingers—aren't meant for violin playing. The opposite was the case when I opened my fifty-year-old sewing machine. I was pleased to find that I could thread it and sew a straight line; maybe I'll have to find something to hone my rusty sewing skills on. We win, and we lose, and we have to concentrate on our victories.

September 18. Today I was searching for my original social security card which I found with other such important items in a lock box. In the box were also things from Bob's billfold, his driver's license, his social security card, Medicare card, and one that identified him as having Parkinson's Disease. The card read, "I have PD which could make me move slowly and have difficulty standing or speaking. I AM NOT INTOXICATED. Please call my family or physician for help." Yes, this was the nature of his condition which was worsening. How he must have suffered, and the family along with him without ever letting on to the depth of our empathy for him. The family and I didn't baby him or pity him, attitudes which would have demeaned him and not strengthened him. We tried so hard to understand and support him—God forgive us if we somehow failed him.

September 23. My morning walk today was to Red Cedar Canyon, a newer development in Hudson filled with lovely homes, natural beauty, and walker friendly paths. I had gotten up thankful for the completely normal results of my annual physical exam yesterday—walking several miles a day is part of my physical and emotional wellness routine. Part way through the canyon I heard the sound of tennis balls bouncing on the court, and then saw a couple walking ahead of me on the path. I couldn't help but think of how wonderful life would have been if Bob could have shared this chapter of life with me. He could have played tennis, we could have enjoyed walks, we would have traveled, spent time with family and friends...on and on. For us, this was not to be, as PD slammed the door shut to that kind of life. Soon I turned my wandering thoughts to the fact that we did have such a great life together, and Bob had many opportunities to savor life with and without me depending on the activity. Again, I told myself, don't be sad because it's over, be glad it happened. Then, almost on cue,

113

an eagle flew overhead, soaring, gliding, free from the troubles of the earth. It had to be Bob telling me to love my life as I'm living it here, and letting me know that he's soaring, free from PD and its debilitating grip on him.

September 28. More inspiration for me to continue writing my story. "It always seems impossible until it's done." Nelson Mandela. "A writer needs experience, observation, and imagination; at any point two can make up for the lack of one." William Faulkner. I'm hoping having the first two will make up for my lack of imagination. And in the words of Katharine Hepburn taken from the book Kate Remembered by A. Scott Berg, "You can't do this and you can't do that, and you could have if you had concentrated and just stuck to it and got to the bottom of it. It's a bit late now, but profit by this—if you do it, do it." I will try to stick to it!

October 7. On "Good Morning America" today, host Robin Roberts said to a guest she was interviewing, "You've reinvented yourself and yet stayed true to who you are—that's not easy to do." There's no better or more succinct way to describe how I've tried to live since Bob died. The loss of my best friend of forty-eight years was devastating, but my choices were to stagnate and wither or to move on and recreate myself. Because I had never lived alone I knew this wouldn't be easy. Foremost was my desire—no, my need—to remain true to who I am. I didn't want to become a spendthrift, neglect my family, be selfish with my time, or falter in my faith in God and the goodness of the world. I also wanted to live so as to honor Bob's memory and insure his legacy.

October 9. In the fall when the leaves change color, I always think of the cycle of the trees. A meteorologist once explained that because of the changes in the amount of sun and of temperature, the chlorophyll that makes leaves green slowly disappears. When it is gone, the leaves show the color that has been underneath the entire season, the gorgeous reds, yellows, oranges, and rusts. I like to think of fall as the time when the trees can show

who they truly are. The old cliché "show your true colo\
lot of meaning for me. When we, like the trees, have expe
the changes of life, we can show our true colors; I like to tl
myself as that warm orange-red of some of the Maples. In this third
chapter of life, we can be bolder and braver in speaking out, in
helping others when needed, indulging our senses, pursuing our
passions, and becoming who we've been since our beginning. Like
the trees in the fall, what a marvelous time.

Most people have a different perspective of the four
seasons than I have. Following fall is winter, the season of old age
in the minds of many. But for me, fall encompasses our senior
years, and winter is the time of gestation, of the bulbs safely
underground and the tree buds inconspicuous, but there. This is the
season of waiting, and waiting, and waiting...until spring comes,
the tenuous, delicate season when the early bloomers can poke their
heads out of the ground only to feel some snowflakes. Sooner or
later summer arrives, bringing warmth, and lots of sunlight and
rainfall, and abundant and welcome growth. Then, often when the
heat is stifling and we tire of summer's oppressiveness, a cool night
or welcome breeze signals that fall is coming again. And with the
new season, a chance for the true colors to show through.

October 13. Friday, October 13, 2017 will mark the
fiftieth anniversary of our engagement. That Friday evening found
us "parked" in a gravel pit near our Luther College campus. Bob
had given me his "brotherhood" pin (Luther didn't have national
fraternities) a year earlier. He started a conversation by saying,
"I've been doing a lot of thinking, and I'm going to have to ask for
my pin back." In the next few seconds of silence, I died a thousand
deaths. Then he quickly added, "In exchange for this", and he held
up a diamond engagement ring. A flood of relief, ecstasy, love, and
commitment were poured into my "yes" amid my tears.

After a while Bob took me back to my campus dormitory,
no co-ed dorms in those days! I hardly slept that night, filled with
excitement as I was. One of my recurring thoughts was that I was

anxious to go to my parents' home to find my grandma's wedding dress. Grandpa L. had given it to me when I was twelve; it was folded and in a plain white box on which he'd written "To Pamela". Grandma L., a seamstress, had made the dress for her wedding in 1911. It was a white, fine linen one with hand embroidered daisies on it. I had never put it on, but had always hoped to be able to wear it at my own wedding. A seamstress made a few alterations so I could wear it June 16, 1968. Grandma and grandpa were able to attend the wedding; I saw them for the moment before grandpa was going to push grandma in her wheelchair into the church. Grandpa had tears in his eyes; was he remembering that day grandma first wore the dress fifty-seven years earlier? The coincidence is that grandma and grandpa had three sons like I went on to have. Time will tell if one of my granddaughters will dare wear the dress and carry on the tradition of having three sons.

October 15 and 16. All day yesterday, my birthday, I kept looking up hoping to see a jet stream which I would have taken as Bob's greeting to me on my special day. To my disappointment I never saw one even though it was a clear, blue sky day. The next morning, I walked out the door at 7:30 am and there was the jet stream! I started crying, realizing that as so often happened, Bob had gotten my birthday on the fifteenth mixed up with our anniversary date of the sixteenth of June. He never was good with dates, a fact he readily admitted, and one year forgot my birthday for about a week. That's when we were living in Carbondale, Illinois, and he remembered my birthday only after questioning why I had been getting so much mail, of course my birthday cards. I saw several more jet streams on the sixteenth, and for good measure he sent a lot of them on the seventeenth, so his lapse on the actual day was quickly forgotten.

October 23. It's been two years since Bob left this life and put himself in God's hands. I thought we would have more years together, but am so thankful for the forty-eight years I knew him. Our first date was fifty years ago this month, a girl-ask-boy Sadie Hawkins dance. He told me months later that he wasn't overly

116

impressed with me after that evening, but thankfully did ask me out again a few weeks later. We had so much fun through the years; now I'm trying to live in ways so that he would give me his big smile and his signature two thumbs up. Rest in peace dear Bob.

October 26. A big thank you to my three sons, daughters-in-law, and grandkids, for making the effort to all be together to celebrate Bob. We didn't even talk much about him, or the date that had just passed, but we all knew he was there in our hearts. I never want any of them to underestimate how much they mean to me as I make my life journey, now without Bob. I look at the faces of the five granddaughters and see, as would be true of the adults also, people who are so bright, so talented, so energetic, and yes, maybe rambunctious. But as Bob and I agreed, we wouldn't have wanted children who "just sat there", seemingly perfect but perhaps lacking in imagination or spunk. I call myself the broken old record who keeps saying "enjoy these years". I ask, and get, my kids' understanding in trying to meet their requests for help, because, while I hate to admit it, I don't have the physical stamina I did even a few years ago. That's maybe age, and my back problems due to scoliosis, and perhaps the stress of recent years. My health is good though, so I keep moving on, with the words of one of my favorite sayings in my head, "Remember, we all stumble, every one of us. That's why it's a comfort to go hand in hand." Thank you, my family, for taking mine.

October 30. Lately I've been thinking a lot about the young woman I was at about seventeen years old, before meeting Bob, and having children, and going through many of the rough times that followed. Can I find my way back to that person, and should I even try? I find myself now in a similar position to that earlier me, on my own, in charge of my life, and the sole decision maker in matters affecting me. I need, and always get, a lot of help from family and friends, but this is not like during the years when I had a spouse or was parenting young children. There's a freedom in this alone state, but also lonesomeness—no one to put to bed at night and no one to climb into bed with. This is chapter three, one

117

in which I'm the only main character. I read recently that the grieving process consists of accepting the loss, working through the pain, adjusting to the environment without the deceased, and finding an enduring connection with the deceased while embarking on a new life. This last step is what I'm working on, the key being "a new life" which is what I must have been seeking by leaving my home of thirty-five years and moving to another city. No one here knew that woman who had short, dark hair, was often with one, two, or three boys, was the one keeping the home fires burning for a husband. Here I'm not someone's daughter, wife, or mother, but only Pam.

November 1, All Saints Day. This afternoon I attended a service commemorating the dead, held by our church in a local cemetery. The service was very meaningful, hearing Scripture passages quoted, and stopping by several graves where we heard the deceased's story read by a family member. As we left the cemetery in solemn procession, I looked upward to see, yes there it was, a jet stream. How can the timing be so perfect in so many instances?

November 13. Friday the thirteenth, always a good day in my opinion. Already several days have passed since Susan Williams, Robin Williams' widow, gave an interview about Robin's last months and his death by suicide. The autopsy performed gave proof that he had Lewy Body Dementia, a more debilitating variant of PD. Not all people affected with PD have dementia, but all with LBD do. No autopsy was ordered for Bob, but I'm convinced that he had the Lewy Body Dementia variant, perhaps the reason that the deep brain stimulation surgery did nothing to improve his PD symptoms. Susan Williams was asked about life with Robin during the last months which she described as a living nightmare. She also answered that Robin was losing his mind, and he knew it. She said Robin's death by suicide was his taking control of his life and saying "NO" to his condition which the interviewer described as devastating. She sadly described how the Robin she knew was slowly fading away, and that his insecurities and paranoia were terrible. I would have given identical answers to every question, and agree with her words that "the wounds won't ever go away, but I've gotten stronger." I have wondered at what cost my strength has been bought, and question if one day I will crumble under the weight of the stress that PD caused.

December 3. One of the most frustrating and heartbreaking aspects of Bob's PD was his hope placed in the results of undergoing deep brain stimulation surgery (DBS). He went to a seminar about DBS, and from that time on he believed this was his only hope of keeping ahead of the progression of his PD. I was opposed to the idea of it, the risks and possible negative side effects, but soon realized my thoughts about it were falling on his deaf ears. Bob called any negativity I voiced as throwing cold water in his face, translated as my taking away his only hope. Finally, I bowed to his insistence.

In April of 2012 he saw a movement disorder specialist, a neurologist trained in diseases such as PD. He deemed Bob a good candidate for DBS, and the march toward it began in earnest. The specialist thought a prime reason for the surgery was that it should allow Bob to quit taking a dopamine agonist which was causing the nasty, and common, side effect of compulsive behaviors. Bob didn't ask if he should gradually taper his dose, but rather went off the medication cold turkey. Unfortunately, he experienced weeks of painful withdrawal; our research at that point informed us that some people can never successfully withdraw from it. During that time, it wasn't unusual for Bob to tell me he thought he would explode, or that he wanted to blow his head off, or to be disoriented and confused. When we took our two-week trip to Norway and Sweden in late May, he continued to be in withdrawal but put up a good front most of the time or sat quietly when he couldn't. Somehow, he made it through the process, only to find that the medication had noticeably alleviated his symptoms; without it his

PD symptoms worsened and responded less well to dopamine replacement.

Before anyone undergoes DBS surgery, extensive testing is done to see if a person is a good candidate for it as it's well known that not all people with PD will benefit from DBS. Any hint of depression rules out a person, and is in fact a possible side effect of having it. Of course, Bob knew this so he hid any sign of depression, and came through all the tests with flying colors. Surgery was scheduled for February, but later postponed until late March causing Bob much anxiety.

During surgery there were already problems, the first being that the surgeon worried that the electrode placed in Bob's brain might be defective since he couldn't get it to function as it should. He removed that electrode and inserted another one; testing at a later date in the lab showed it was perfect. Bob was awake for the duration of the surgery so he could respond to directions the surgeon gave him and give feedback about feelings he experienced. He repeatedly said he had a terrible sensation in his left leg, one strong enough that he could barely tolerate it. The feeling subsided when the stimulation was turned off and then left off, standard procedure for the first weeks following surgery. Bob's overall good health gave him a speedy recovery, and after the generator, or battery, was placed in his chest, he was discharged from the hospital on Good Friday, March 29, 2013.

We arrived home in Barron on Saturday, the day before Easter. Bob was feeling good and wanted to take a short walk. We stopped by Pastor Lori's house and had a short visit with her and her husband. All of us cried and hugged, relieved that the surgery was over and had, despite its problems, gone well according to the surgeon. Bob had a large scar on his head, but that didn't prevent his attending church on Easter Sunday. Bob had been a long-time member of the church choir, sadly quitting only when his voice became too unpredictable because of PD. A tradition at our church was to invite anyone in the congregation to join the choir in singing the "Hallelujah Chorus" from Handel's "Messiah". Bob knew this well, so when invited he joined the rest of us in the choir in singing this amazing anthem. As he walked back to his pew he received a round of applause—what a support group this was.

Bob enjoyed a few days when he looked and acted much like his old self. This is referred to as the "honeymoon period" after DBS surgery, unexplained by common sense or medical knowledge because there is no stimulation being sent to the brain. Bob's first session with the programmer—the person trained in the subtleties of electrical stimulation—was scheduled for two weeks after the surgery. The results were inconclusive as any stimulation that made a difference in PD symptoms gave Bob the same intolerable leg sensations that he felt during surgery. This was the first of many disappointing programming sessions, the next one set for two months in the future. That one produced no better results, and Bob left with the device again turned off and the doctor declaring he thought it unlikely the stimulation would ever work. While this blunt assessment was devastating to us, we still held out hope for positive results in the future.

Two days after this appointment was our forty-fifth wedding anniversary, the last one we spent together. Because Bob felt worse with the stimulation completely off, he asked me to restart it at the level where it had been before being turned off at the clinic two days before. We had been given instructions and freedom to do this, and both of us thought it would be helpful to try it. Bob had a few hours of feeling close to normal, so we celebrated the day by going to dinner with my cousin and his wife. In the old days, people often celebrated a forty-fifth anniversary in a big way, thinking they would never reach their fiftieth. We should have done the same.

John and Jenna had planned their wedding for June 29, 2013 a year earlier, so knowing this we had scheduled surgery accordingly, assuming that Bob would be a new person three months afterward, ready to talk, smile, eat, and dance like he once did. Even though we had left the stimulation turned on, most of the time it made no difference. He took medication every two hours, but after about only one hour it started to wear off and he suffered all the usual difficulties with slowness of movement, barely audible voice, swallowing, and some mental fog. He took extra pills and made it through the ceremony, dinner, and reception, but then said he would have to leave. Missing the dance would have broken our hearts, so I said I would help him use the outdoor toilet hoping that would mean we could stay a little longer. Accomplishing this wasn't easy in a small space with his need for me to get his pants down, help with the toileting, and then redress him. Like the other men in the wedding party, he wore Dockers pants with suspenders, a white shirt, and necktie. But we succeeded, and then were able to enjoy a few dances before saying our good-byes to everyone. What a wonderful time it was.

Shortly before the wedding we had started looking for options of other clinics Bob could go to in search of a different programmer. One such place highly recommended was in the Cities, a Parkinson's specialty clinic. We made an appointment for a month ahead with renewed hope for good results. Starting at a new clinic meant going through a lot of testing again, and answering many questions by staff about why we wanted to change programmers mid-stream, not commonly done. This programmer, a woman bubbling with smiles and positivity, promised she would "work her magic" by changing some of the intricate settings on the four points of the implanted electrode. After this appointment, we left elated and excited. But even before we arrived home Bob felt over stimulated, slept poorly that night, and by morning we were driving the two hours back to have the settings readjusted lower. We made an appointment for a month in the future.

Between appointments at this clinic, Bob had a single car accident. He was driving alone to Rice Lake, taking what was for him the unusual route by way of the interstate. The accident report stated that he left the freeway, traveled in the ditch along the highway, and then crashed at high speed into a tree. He told the investigating officer that he wasn't wearing his seat belt, another aberration from normal. He was taken by helicopter to the hospital in Eau Claire where a complete checkup revealed that the only damage was a cracked sternum caused by the deployed airbag. Was this his first attempt at suicide? We never knew, he never said it was, rather talking about having had some kind of dizzy spell which can happen to those with PD because of a sudden change in blood pressure. He did say several times after the accident that there "must be a reason I'm still here."

At the second appointment at the specialty clinic, the doctor concentrated on what could have caused Bob's recent accident. Perhaps he suspected Bob was depressed and that it had been a suicide attempt or a call for help. He tweaked the medication a bit, but the programmer who saw us that day left the electrode settings as they were; this time there was no promise of using any magic. Yet another visit that left us deflated and growing increasingly less hopeful that Bob would see that the surgery had been successful. He was now more than four months past the surgery, a long enough period that he should have seen what for many who undergo it call miraculous results.

Bob's appointment with yet a fourth programmer was not one we originated. We received a phone call from the surgeon's secretary saying he was so sorry that he hadn't followed up with Bob sooner. Had he maybe heard about the accident, or perhaps learned from one or the other of the two clinics that Bob wasn't responding well to stimulation? Of course, we scheduled the appointment as he requested, thinking that this time the doctor and the programmer would find the optimum settings. The surgeon was a very personable, outgoing man who greeted Bob the way he always did with an outstretched hand and "Hello Dr. Oman." Prior to the office visit, Bob had undergone another MRI to make certain the electrode was still where it had been placed during surgery. Given that this was the case, the doctor promised that finding the right amount of stimulation would be possible and that Bob would be his old self. Present at this appointment was the doctor, a programmer, and a representative of the company that made the stimulation device. The latter two were as positive as the doctor that THIS time the right settings would be found. They started changing the settings, as mentioned before a highly-complicated process, and soon Bob was able to jog down the hall. He was grinning from ear to ear, laughing, talking easily—truly the man I once knew. I will never forget those exciting moments!

We were told to go have some lunch and come back in about an hour. But already, Bob was experiencing the horrible feelings which he couldn't accurately describe, but by now knew all too well. This time he said he felt like he "wanted to go jump off a bridge." We don't want you to do that the doctor said, and once more the stimulation was turned lower, thus making it ineffective. Right back to square one, no progress. The highs and lows, the hopes raised and then dashed, wore more heavily on us at each session, now numbering five.

We had one more appointment at this clinic, with yet a different doctor who was a Parkinson's specialist, and the same programmer. This time there was no company rep and no bright promises from anyone about what to expect. It felt to us like Bob was being abandoned, and maybe that is what truly was happening. He was exactly where he was after the two appointments with the first programmer who, while we didn't want to accept it then, was probably correct—the DBS surgery was not ever going to prove effective for Bob. This was two days before Bob's death.

In the years since then I've had time to reflect on his death by suicide. The words of Peter Shaw who ended his life September 17, 2015, are eerily similar to what I am certain Bob would have written in a last note if there had been one. Peter wrote, "I am sane, quite good humored, and not at all depressed. Why then am I doing this? Because I am rational, and in my present condition suicide is rational. I have had a good life, and prolonging it will not make it better. Senility is setting in fast. My mind doesn't work as well or as quickly as it used to, and it is getting worse day by day. My physical and mental vigor are reduced, and life is an effort. I am not afraid of dying but I am afraid of pain and incompetence, and I don't believe palliative care will be sufficient." His wife Pat quoted his having said several times that "having seen my two sisters die in nursing homes, I have no wish to go that way." For Bob, it had been watching his mother and his sister languish in nursing homes, one because of recurring strokes and the other because of fluid accumulation in the brain's ventricles.

January 2, 2016, back to the present after reviewing Bob's experience with DBS surgery. Yesterday, to celebrate the new year, Jenna had a list of questions that she asked John and me. They were about the year past and the year to come. One was, "What was a hard lesson you learned last year?" I didn't hesitate before I answered that I've learned the hole in my heart made by the loss of Bob will never heal. At times, I miss him so much; looking at pictures can be a painful, tearful process, but also one laced with humor and thoughts of what a full, good, life we had together. Only the last years were sadder and more complicated because of Bob's PD. We both tried hard to be upbeat, but it was less and less possible as the PD progressed. Bob had to deal with his deteriorating condition, and the pain for me was seeing this happen to him. Time might dissipate the harshness of the last months by helping erase the rough memories and bring the good memories into sharper focus. Then it's those good memories that trigger the lonesomeness, and the cycle begins again.

It's probably true that we can't know what effect a loss will have on us until we experience the loss. I would not have predicted the depth and breadth, the multi-dimensional nature of Bob's loss on me. We're told that everyone grieves in his or her own way, and that there is no right or wrong timetable for grief. I question whether I have given myself much chance to grieve, but rather have filled my days with activity, moving to a new city, helping take care of my mom, and then selling her home and things...run, Pam, run, then grief can't catch you. As I'm typing, I hear a news reporter talking about how Prince Harry failed to deal with his mother's, Princess Diana's, death for twenty years. To protect himself from her loss at age twelve, he cut himself off from feeling all emotion and fell into depression. He has only recently sought and gotten professional help, and now wants to tell his story so that others can benefit from it.

January 5. In my hospice volunteer role, I'm currently visiting a lady once a week around noon when her Meals on Wheels is delivered. Her family hopes that having someone with her at meal time will encourage her to eat. The plan is working well, at least on the days I've been there; my challenge is turning down some of the food she offers me so that she gets enough. Yesterday I asked her as a one-hundred-year-old lady if she had a favorite time of her life. She thought for a minute or two and then said, "I can't really say that one time is a favorite. I've sort of taken each time as it comes, and they're all mostly good." What a terrific attitude, and what a lesson for me to take into the new year. I will continue to try to live each day as it comes and enjoy them all.

January 13. On the advice of mom's care takers at the memory care home, we placed her in hospice care today. She can remain where she is living, a blessing as moving her would be traumatic for her. There's been no significant change in her health status, but her dementia has rapidly progressed making it difficult to know how she's feeling or if she has any pain. While my brothers and I hope it's not the case, we wonder if the fact that she's been on an anti-depressant for two weeks is also causing confusion, dizziness, and a couple of falls. Initially her doctor wasn't in favor of writing a prescription for this, but after being pressed by the care givers, he wrote one. We siblings didn't argue with this, agreeing that we aren't the ones who have to take care of her. She can be difficult and combative at times, so different from how she would normally be. My brothers and I have found that having the Power of Attorney for Health Care for another person is a tough job—should there be treatments, or medicines prescribed, or therapy initiated? By placing her in hospice we have put mom's care totally in the hands of professionals, hopefully the right decision for her now.

January 25. This is Chuck's seventy-second birthday, another reminder of the rapidly passing years as he's my oldest friend in terms of how long I've known him. Also, today two people drew my attention to a new book titled <u>When Breath Becomes Air</u>, written by a thirty-seven-year-old doctor who learned he had terminal lung cancer. Anyone who's read it can't talk about it without becoming emotional. Already under his death sentence, he and his wife decided to have a baby. She was born a few months before he died, and he called her "air becoming breath". His description of death and birth as being the same process in opposite directions echoes my thoughts; this belief makes our beginning and our ending more alike than opposite. The book is next on my reading list.

January 28. More and more often these days, a topic of conversation for my friends and me is death, our own or someone else's. As we witness the end of life for others, we ponder our own death. Without fail, everyone I've talked with agrees that a life lived too long, as in my mom's demented state, is not desirable. The length of life does not override the quality of life. What Bob, and Robin Williams, and the previously mentioned Peter Shaw were preventing by their deaths by suicide was the nightmare of living with an impaired, or worse, a non-functioning, brain. They saw the train wreck coming and had to jump off before it happened. Those I've spoken with, and I, don't know if we could choose to die, but we understand the correctness of those who have had sound reason to do so. Perhaps within the next decades there will be less stigma associated with "chosen death" and also access to doctors who can assist with carrying out their wishes.

February 21. This weekend I was in Hayward to watch Andy and John finish another Birkebeiner cross country ski race. I've been at every one of the finish lines since Andy started skiing them several years ago, John following soon after. My heart skips a couple of beats as each one crosses, knowing they have worked hard and done their best. We experienced the same skip a beat moment when Matt handed us the letter informing him that he had passed his Professional Engineer test the first time he took it; with his usual sense of humor this was only after he first showed us a letter stating he had missed passing it by one point. It's not win or lose that's important, but rather knowing that your child did his best. Before I left this weekend, I had made certain that my Eau Claire brothers and wives would be in town to monitor mom's condition. Sunday night I found out by phone that she'd had a rough weekend, had eaten little, slept a lot, and appeared to be nearing death.

February 22. Today, Monday, I spent several hours with mom. One of the workers was saddened to learn that mom had barely eaten all weekend as she'd seemed quite herself when the worker had last seen her on Thursday. We propped her up in bed and fed her some ice cream and a few spoonsful of Ensure. She never said my name, but did ask for her "mama" and sister Glady. She was more lucid when I left than when I arrived, but I also thought death was creeping up on her. After giving her a kiss and saying I love you, I promised I'd be back on Thursday.

February 24. As I was finishing our church's Wednesday night Lenten supper, Paul called to tell me mom had just passed. There were lots of people around to give me their sympathy and hugs; I have no idea what those without such great support groups do in times of sorrow or pain. I was glad I had spent a good, long day with mom on Monday, trying but not succeeding in staving off the inevitable. Rest in peace mom, nana as the grandchildren call her. She died having lived ninety-two years and nearly eight months, almost exactly the same age at which her mother and only sibling, her sister, died.

February 25. My brothers and sisters-in-law, Andy, the undertaker, minister, and I met today at the funeral home to plan mom's service. We know she would want a very traditional visitation at the funeral home, service at her church across the street, and burial in the plot next to my dad. They had purchased a plot and gravestone several years before my dad died so we didn't have to make any choices about those matters. We wrote the obituary, and Andy said he would make the video collage of pictures which I had gathered for him to use. The rest of us will make "memory boards" to showcase her long and useful life and bring a few items near and dear to her to the funeral home. There's therapy in being together, laughing, crying, and remembering a life.

March 5. Yesterday was the celebration of life for mom, our modern term for funeral. We did celebrate her life, remembering her love for all of us, her church, her home and cabin, and her ability to tell stories that went on and on. We had chosen Bible verses and hymns that we knew she would have approved. The day was cold, rainy, a bit snowy, rather appropriate for a funeral. Now she's resting next to my dad and under a large Norway Pine tree. On the gravestone are my parents' names, the words parents of and the names of their four children, and my dad's favorite, "Takk for alt", thanks for everything.

March 30. There is much I haven't written about that has been a large part of my life. I haven't penned any words about my thoughts about politics, or about the fact that since I was about ten years old I've considered myself to be on the world's board of directors, even though there is no such board. I worried myself sick through such world crises as the ones about the Suez Canal (1956), the US invasion of Lebanon (1958), several Berlin confrontations, the islands of Quemoy and Matsu (1960), the Cuban missile crisis (1962), and on and on. I remember thinking that it was an exercise in futility to sign up for classes in high school because the world would be destroyed by then, the fall of 1961. But in 1989, miraculously, the Berlin Wall fell, and there began a sea change in world politics. My cousin's son was in Berlin at that time and brought back chunks of the cement wall that had divided the world between Communist and Free. I keep our piece as a reminder of the power that people who resist can have.

Slowly the Cold War thawed, the world breathed a collective sigh of relief, and there was a time when I fell asleep not worrying about what the morning's news would bring. This was when our sons were ten, thirteen, and eighteen, and we could see a relatively stable and bright future for them. But then, like a bolt of lightning, we woke to the horrible news of the September 11 attacks. From then on, terrorist activities, all the minor wars that could become major ones, climate change and what it may mean for the earth, the polarization of our country along so many lines of divide, and on and on...threaten us.

I've written some about my faith, which I have struggled with and pondered almost daily. I am always comforted by the verse that my nephew chose for his confirmation of faith day, Psalm 94:19: "When doubts fill my mind and my heart is filled with doubt, Quiet me and give me renewed hope and cheer." My faith rests in a God, a supreme being of love and intelligence and mercy, who is the web holding all of creation together. Alfred, Lord Tennyson, expressed a similar thought in these inspiring words: "I can but trust that good shall fall, At last—far off—at last, to all, And every winter change to spring." I believe the churches or religions that will survive are those that offer God's love and peace freely, without price, to all people.

My thoughts about death have appeared at times in my writing, partly because of my age, but also because the very structure of my chapter three life has been determined by Bob's and my mom's deaths. For the first time in my life I'm living alone, widowed and orphaned, and not a care taker for anyone. While I can't say that death is my friend, it is no longer a stranger to me nor an enemy. I now see so clearly that every life, no matter how short or long, has meaning and affects other lives; the ripples that each life creates reach distant shores. When we die we become a part of the universe and are, as we always have been, in God's hands. I may wish to have one more day on earth no matter how old I become, but I won't fear for what will happen to me when I die. I'd like to believe that I will be one of those stars whose light is yet visible even though the physical entity which produced the light is gone. The beautiful metaphor for death is the one Pastor Steve used at Bob's funeral: "Death isn't extinguishing a lamp; it's more like turning off a night light because the morning has arrived."

April 20. Today my thoughts centered on Olaf Stavrum, the Norwegian immigrant who came to Hudson, lived, died, and was buried here in the Willow River Cemetery, founded in 1850. I was asked by a distant cousin of Bob's who lives in Norway to find his grave to show his visiting great granddaughters. They and their husbands were a delightful foursome who were so appreciative of my efforts to find his grave and the house, still occupied, he and his wife had lived in.

The story these women told me was much like those of the hundreds of immigrants from many countries who have come to America for centuries. Olaf first came to America in 1910 and returned home to Norway, determined to come back to live here permanently. By 1913 he had found the woman he wanted to marry and promised her a new life in America. She, however, would not leave Norway, and even though, unbeknownst to Olaf, she was pregnant with his child, she stayed behind. Olaf found another woman, Hannah, who he did marry and who emigrated with him. He never saw or knew of the son born to the woman in Norway, nor did he have any children with Hannah. Their lives made me think of the depth of the heartache for both those who left and those who stayed behind in the homeland. Their story also highlights the strength of the dream of those who left so much in one country in order to find what they hoped would be a better life in a new country.

April 22. This is Earth Day, the day we celebrate the beauty and resources of the earth, our only home. Gaylord Nelson of Wisconsin first declared an Earth Day in 1970, a day I remember

131

well. I was teaching seventh grade English and Reading in the St. Anthony Village school system. Bob and I had recently found out that we would be moving to Carbondale, Illinois to pursue our master's degrees. It was a daunting move for us as we'd never lived that far from our families. We've always been environmentally conscious, trying our best to appreciate the earth and be kind to it even when being so wasn't in vogue. The only song I ever composed was written for a long-ago Earth Day; I can still play the tune on the piano, but I've forgotten many of the words. I can recall the last ones which were, "And now that we dare to dream small dreams of hope, may we live so they all may come true." That remains my hope decades later.

May 10. Suddenly today I felt a little of the fear that Bob must have been living with all the time. My physical problems are rather minor but worrisome. I continue to search for the cause of a rash on my forearms and a few other places; visits to three doctors have not found a reason. I have some pain and lack of mobility as I wait for my scheduled hip replacement surgery, necessitated by arthritic deterioration of the joint. I'm not as flexible as I was, and I tire more easily when active. My scoliosis is part of the problem and will never get better, perhaps only worse with time. I'm forced to contemplate what my physical state will be like in the future— what will my abilities and limitations be? These questions were not only worries for Bob, they had become his reality. No wonder he was so frustrated and weakened in spirit as well as body. And as his body fell apart, his ability to participate in life diminished. Now I can begin to imagine the depth of his fear for his future.

May 24. Maya Angelou, as only she can write, said of those who've died and those who grieve, "And when great souls die, after a period peace blooms, slowly and always irregularly. Spaces fill with a kind of soothing electric vibration. Our senses, restored, never to be the same, whisper to us. They existed. They existed. We can be. Be and be better. For they existed."

May 26. The book <u>Me Before You</u>, written by Jojo Moyes, resonated with me like none other, perhaps the reason Sarah said I had to read it. In the beginning of the book, the main character Will is hit by a car on his way to work, and as a result is a quadriplegic. Other people had a hard time understanding Will's feelings about his life as a quadriplegic, but he expressed them this way: "I loved my life. Really loved it. I loved my job, my travels, the things I was. I loved being a physical person...I led a big life." Later in this conversation with his care giver who has fallen in love with him, and he with her, he says: "I don't want you to be tied to me, to my hospital appointments, to the restrictions on my life. I don't want you to miss out on many things. And, selfishly, I don't want you to look at me one day and feel even the tiniest bit of regret or pity. I can't be the kind of man who just...accepts." Could these have been Bob's thoughts when he wrote in his journal in the last days of his life, "I love Pam so much I don't know what to do."

Will's medical care giver Nathan, a professional, was realistic in assessing Will's choice about wanting to end his life. He summed up his opinion this way: "I want him to live if he wants to live. If he doesn't, then by forcing him to carry on, you, me— no matter how much we love him—we become just another shitty bunch of people taking away his choices." Later, care giver Louisa finally realizes, "what has been the worst thing for him has been losing the ability to make a single decision, to do a single thing for himself."

A poignant reminder of an incident in Bob's and my life was the scene in which Will and Louisa were attending the wedding of Will's ex-girlfriend. Louisa said of Will, "he could be happy...if allowed to be Will, instead of The Man in the Wheelchair, the list of symptoms, the object of pity." Then Louisa sat in Will's lap, and he moved the wheelchair to the beat of the music. This was like our night at John and Jenna's wedding, when first John danced ne, Jenna danced with her dad, and then Bob and I danced. ere just two people, dancing, Bob not being defined by his Parkinson's, nor the object of pity, nor his list of symptoms, just Bob. What a joyful memory.

June 6. "It has been said, 'Time heals all wounds.' I do not agree. The wounds remain. In time, the mind, protecting its sanity, covers the wounds with scar tissue and the pain lessens. But it's never gone." Those are Rose Kennedy's words; she knew how to describe grief and loss, and experienced more of it than most of us have. Her words revealed why I reacted with gut wrenching sadness to the death of Muhammad Ali, the famous boxer who endured the ravages of PD for more than thirty years. A replay of TV's Ed Bradley's piece about him made twenty years ago highlighted how much Ali had failed in the years of his life after his PD diagnosis. The vivid memories of Bob's last months came flooding back as I watched the interview with this once world class athlete, so weakened he could often not speak nor walk, only slowly shuffle. My wounds caused by Bob's condition and then his death have healed a little; the edges are a bit less raw as scar tissue has formed, but the hole in my heart will always be there.

The tributes to Ali highlighted the fact that he wanted no pity for his PD. He was at times embarrassed by how diminished he was, but didn't want people to feel sorry for him. Yet again here was what plagued me with Bob's PD. I resolutely refused to pity him even though I could see how he was suffering, how embarrassed he could sometimes feel, and how PD so affected his quality of life. I kept up the brave front right up to the end, telling him the night before he died how proud I was of him for going to the area dinner meeting for city utility commissioners. He said, "Can't you see what a mess I am?", but I wouldn't agree with him, only tried to bolster the small amount of self-confidence he had left.

June 16. Some days our learning curve is steeper than others, much steeper. One such day for me was this one, my forty-eighth wedding anniversary, and the day I left the hospital after having hip replacement surgery two days ago. What started dawning on me was the difference to my chapter three life this surgery might make. Because the hip was very deteriorated, my precipitous slope to the left side has been due more to the hip than to my scoliosis. Having gained close to an inch in height with the new hip, I should be more level than I've been since I was a teenager—I need to encourage the left side muscles to stretch to accommodate my new height, all 5' 2 1/2" of it!

I hadn't been home for long today when I sat down to play the piano, a favorite pastime of mine. I played Canon in D which has such a lovely, majestic cadence throughout. There are however some very fast notes which have always given me problems. For the first time, I decided to count 1 and, 2 and, 3 and, faithfully. The more I played, the better I played, and the easier it was to play, proof that nothing improves without practice, practice, practice.

Later in the day I turned on the radio to my go-to station, WCCO. Airing was an interview with a man whose name I can't remember, who wrote a book whose title I can't remember, about our presidents and what kind of fathers they were. What struck me most was the author's comment about Abraham Lincoln, who after the death of his son, was able to "reach deep inside himself to find new strength and energy". He added that for some presidents, tragedy brought them low, never to recover. I have to wonder if through some miracle of personality, circumstances, my faith, and my supportive family and friends, I could do like Lincoln and reach deep inside myself after Bob's suicide. I will never lose that picture of him lifeless that morning of October 23, but I was able to keep going, start thriving again, and find a new energy and beauty in life. I will always be thankful for the gift that allowed me to do this.

June 17. Today I learned my last life lesson in these two days as I walked slowly around my small yard. We've had abundant rain so the grass is doing well, but so are the weeds. Now that I'm "convalescing" I can't stoop down to pull the weeds. So, Pam, I told myself, get over the idea of perfection, which is never a part of this life anyway, and accept with gratitude what I have. I own a home surrounded by a yard on a street with friendly neighbors protected by good authorities, plenty to eat in this home, and family and friends in abundance—why care about a few weeds?

August 8. (8/8/16) Rather a nice date I thought when I wrote it. Finally, there were lots of jet streams today after a couple of weeks of my not seeing any. I wonder what Bob already knows? Or maybe he is only putting an exclamation point on my ideas of the last two days, ideas about fear and what it can do to people. The pastor's sermon yesterday focused on a verse from Luke 12, later expanded on in a hymn. The words in it are those of Jesus when he said, "Have no fear little flock." Such simple words, but what a profound statement. Issues of safety infuse much of our modern life: are the car seats safe, is the drinking water safe, are my credit and identity safe, the list continues on, slightly different for each of us and for every generation, but important to all.

Another somewhat less personal level of fear is heightened by the media and political figures. In this presidential election year, we are told every day that we're not safe in America, that we should live in fear of many of our neighbors because of color, or race, or religion, or gender orientation. Some politicians prey on this fear, promising that he or she or one political party or the other is the only savior from the sources of our fear. President Franklin Roosevelt recognized the power of fear when he said in his 1933 inaugural address, "Let me assert my firm belief that the only thing we have to fear is fear itself—nameless, unreasoning, unjustified terror." Bertrand Russell understood the power of fear saying, "Neither a man nor a crowd nor a nation can be trusted to act humanely or to think sanely under the influence of great fear."

The reality is that no worldly person or power or party can save us from what we fear, but rather our trust in God who promises to be with us no matter what happens. The truth is that because of the laws of nature and the sins of mankind, bad things will happen, over and over. There will be wars and floods and diseases and hard economic times and car accidents and all manner of disasters. But we need not live a life of fear. We can trust that whatever befalls us, we are being held in the web of God's love and mercy.

October 15. Now I am living out Chapter Three of my life. Since I'm entering my eighth decade today, one might ask what I mean by Chapter Three. Chapter One began in 1946 and included my childhood, teen years, college, and early years of marriage through the birth of our three sons. When my youngest son was six months old, I was thirty-three, and we moved to Barron. That ended Chapter One. Chapter Two covered the thirty-five years we lived in Barron, Bob and I raising our sons to adulthood, working hard to support our family and provide for our future, becoming empty nesters, and beginning retirement. The last years of the second chapter were dominated by Bob's Parkinson's Disease and his efforts to live within its increasingly serious limitations.

Leaving Barron at age sixty-seven several months after Bob's death distinctly marked the beginning of Chapter Three. Without looking back, I put the final period on the last sentence of Chapter Two. I have rarely questioned my decision to start over in this vibrant city, living alone for the first time in my life, but closer to my sons and families. My job now is to make certain I am giving back to the world what I have so generously been given. I try to smile more and seldom frown, to smell the roses rather than rush by them, to by attitude and example love my neighbor as myself, and leave as small a footprint on the earth as possible. Once in a while it's harder than usual to get out of bed in the morning, but then I give myself a talk about the beauty of the world and the goodness of the people in it.

Long ago a famous theologian was asked what he would do if he thought the world was going to end the next day. He responded, "I'd plant a tree." With that as inspiration, I will do my best to plant my trees, keep on walking, and doing unto others. I can live, as Bob died on that October 23, in the sure and certain knowledge that no matter what dark valley I walk through, God is with me as He is with everyone. I know that "In our end is our beginning; in our time, infinity; in our doubt there is believing; in our life, eternity. In our death, a resurrection; at the last, a victory." (From "Hymn of Promise" by Natalie Sleeth)

Epilogue

For my epilogue, I could find, yet again, no more fitting words than what have already been written. In the epilogue of Kristin Hannah's book <u>Winter Garden</u>, the main character Vera says:

"I cannot help smiling as I close this book—my book. After all these years, I have finished my journal. Not a fairy tale, not a pretense; my story, as true as I can tell it. My father would be proud of me. I am a writer at last.

It is my gift to my daughters, although they have given so much more to me, and without them, of course, these words would still be trapped inside, poisoning me from within."

I would only change the words "my daughters" to my husband, my sons, and daughters-in-law. And so, with echoes of my dad's Norwegian-accented tenor voice and Bob's resonant baritone, "Takk for alt." Thanks for everything!

Words of Wisdom from Others

Grief is just love with no place to go. --Jamie Anderson

If God speaks to us at all in this world, if God speaks anywhere, it is into our personal lives...through our individual 'sacred stories.' --Friedrich Buechner

Saint Theresa's Prayer

> May today there be peace within.

> May you trust God that you are exactly where you are meant to be.

> May you not forget the infinite possibilities that are born of faith.

> May you use those gifts you have received, and pass on the love that has been given to you.

> May you be content knowing you are a child of God.

> Let this presence settle into your bones, and allow your soul the freedom to sing, dance, praise, and love.

> It is there for each and every one of us.

We leave behind a bit of ourselves wherever we've been. --Edmond Harcourt

Do your little bit of good where you are; it's those little bits of good put together that overwhelm the world. --Desmond Tutu

There are many compliments that may come to an individual in the course of a lifetime, but there is no higher tribute than to be loved by those who know us best. --Rev. Dale Turner

There is not less wit nor less invention in applying rightly a thought one finds in a book than in being the first author of that thought. --Pierre Bayle

I don't know what your destiny will be, but one thing I do know: the only ones among you who will be really happy are those who have sought and found how to serve. --Albert Schweitzer

I am only one/But still I am one/I cannot do everything/But still I can do something/And because I cannot do everything/I will not refuse to do the something that I can do. --Edward Everett Hale

One day, in retrospect, the years of struggle will strike you as the most beautiful. --Sigmund Freud

I long to accomplish a great and noble task, but it is my chief duty to accomplish humble tasks as though they were great and noble. The world is moved along, not only by the mighty shoves of its heroes, but also by the aggregate of the tiny pushes of each honest worker. --Helen Keller

Writing is like driving a car at night. You can only see as far as the headlights, but you make the whole trip that way. --E.L. Doctorow

If only I may grow, firmer, simpler, quieter, warmer.
--Dag Hammarskjold

Life is an adventure in forgiveness. --Norman Cousins

Too often we underestimate the power of a touch, a smile, a kind word, a listening ear, an honest compliment, or the smallest act of caring, all of which have the potential to turn a life around.
--Leo Buscaglia

Imagine there's no countries/It isn't hard to do/Nothing to kill or die for/No religion too/Imagine all the people/living in peace.
--John Lennon

Every man has his secret sorrows, which the world knows not; and often times we call a man cold when he is only sad.
--Henry Wadsworth Longfellow

Good fiction creates empathy. A novel takes you somewhere and asks you to look through the eyes of another person, to live another life. --Barbara Kingslover

As I have not worried to be born, I do not worry to die.
--Federico Garcia Lorca

Everybody needs his memories. They keep the wolf of insignificance from the door. --Saul Bellow

The pages are still blank, but there is a miraculous feeling of the words being there, written in invisible ink and clamoring to become visible. --Vladimir Nabokov

Use the talents you possess, for the woods would be a very silent place if no birds sang except the best. --Henry Van Dyke

We are all broken, that's how the light gets in.
--Ernest Hemingway

All living creatures are sparks from the radiation of God's brilliance, and these sparks emerge from God like the rays of the sun...through them the divine flame is visible.
--Hildegard of Bingen

> Do you wish the world were happy?
>
> Then remember day by day
>
> Just to scatter seeds of kindness as you pass along the way.
>
> --Ella Wilcox

You never really understand a person until you consider things from his point of view. --Harper Lee

I slept and dreamt that life was joy. I woke and saw that life was service. I acted and behold, service was joy.
--Robindranath Tagore

The bitterest tears shed over graves are for words left unsaid and deeds left undone. --Harriet Beecher Stowe

True religion is the life we lead, not the creed we profess.
--Louis Nizer

The life of every man is a diary in which he means to write one story, and writes another, and his humblest hour is when he compares the volume as it is with what he vowed to make it.
--J.M. Barrie

If you want to work on your art, work on your life.
--Anton Chekov

Words are things; and a small drop of ink/Falling like dew upon a thought, produces/That which makes thousands, perhaps millions, think. --Lord Byron

Science is organized knowledge. Wisdom is organized life.
--Immanuel Kant

My life is my message. --Mohandas Gandhi

Books are the compasses and extants and charts which other men have prepared to help us navigate the dangerous seas of human life. --Jesse Bennett

It's a bit embarrassing to have been concerned with the human problem all one's life and find at the end that we have no more to offer by way of advice than "try to be a little kinder."
--Aldous Huxley

Perhaps the best cure for the fear of death is to reflect that life has a beginning as well as an end. There was a time when you were not that gives us no concern. Why then should it trouble us that a time will come when we shall cease to be? To die is only to be as we were before we were born. --William Hazlitt

What do we live for, if it is not to make life less difficult for each other? --George Eliot (Mary Ann Evans)

The greatest happiness of life is the conviction that we are loved—loved for ourselves, or rather, loved in spite of ourselves. --Victor Hugo

When you turn the corner/And you run into yourself/Then you know that you have turned/All the corners that are left. --Langston Hughes

If you write to impress it will always be bad, but if you write to express it will be good. --Thornton Wilder

Love all, trust a few, do wrong to none. --William Shakespeare

There are a thousand thoughts lying within a man that he does not know til he takes up a pen to write. --William Thackeray

The art of life is to know how to enjoy a little and to endure much. --William Hazlitt

As we advance in life it becomes more and more difficult, but in fighting the difficulties the inmost strength of the heart is developed. --Vincent Van Gogh

We must learn to regard people less in the light of what they do or omit to do, and more in the light of what they suffer. --Dietrich Bonhoeffer

The simplest questions are the most profound. Where were you born? Where is your home? Where are you going? What are you doing? Think about these once in awhile and watch your answers change. --Richard Bach

One of the oldest human needs is having someone wonder where you are when you don't come home at night. --Margaret Mead

The greatest part of a writer's time is spent in reading in order to write. --Samuel Johnson

The pursuit of truth and beauty is a sphere of activity in which we are permitted to remain children all our lives. --Albert Einstein

In small matters trust the mind, in the large ones the heart. --Sigmund Freud

The world is round and the place which may seem like the end may also be only the beginning. --George Baker (1877-1965)

Unless someone like you cares a whole awful lot, nothing is going to get better. It's not. --Dr. Seuss

The only gift is a portion of thyself. --Ralph Waldo Emerson

I'd rather see a sermon than hear one any day; I'd rather one should walk with me than merely tell the way. --Edgar Guest

We are healed of a suffering only by expressing it to the full. --Marcel Proust

Heavy hearts, like heavy clouds in the sky, are but relieved by the letting of a little water. --Christopher Marley

Here's the test to find whether your mission on earth is finished: if you're alive, it isn't. --Richard Bach

The greatest thing about growing older is that you don't lose all the other ages you've been. --Madeleine L'Engle

In death the many become one; in life the one become many. --Robindranath Tagore